HOW TO BE A GOOD BAD BOY

Becoming the Man That Women Really Desire

By

Jeff d'Avanzo

Copyright © 2012 Jeff d'Avanzo

All rights reserved.

ISBN: **0615652611**
ISBN-13: 97806156526109

CONTENTS

	Acknowledgments	i
	Preface	iii
1	The Good and Bad of Being Mr. Nice Guy	1
2	Understanding Venusian	28
3	Seducing Women the Good Bad Boy Way	48
4	Becoming a Seduction Artist	62
5	Kissing and Keeping Your Balance	75
6	The Power of Your (In)Actions	86
7	Becoming A Good Bad Boy	101
8	Evolving as a Good Bad Boy	115
9	Becoming the Good Bad Boyfriend/Husband	130

ACKNOWLEDGMENTS

I'd like to express my gratitude to Dr. Angela Aiello for her help in delineating and describing the different types of real Bad Boys, as well as her encouragement in getting this book done.

Jeff d'Avanzo

PREFACE

In the past I would always be dumbfounded by how the lovely, sexy women that I knew in my life would always seem to end up in relationships with bad guys that I knew weren't very good for them--not the caring, respectful guy that I was!

I was a decent, attractive enough guy, but never could seem to easily get the intimate attentions of women. I started asking the women I knew about this and they spoke of the allure and raw attraction of a Bad Boy, but how treacherous they were to deal with due to their general emotional unavailability, among other unsavory attributes. I spent a lot of time after that pushing back the boundaries of my Nice Guy and letting the Bad Boy inside me get much more presence in intimate situations--experimenting--which was a revelation to me with wonderful results with women. It became obvious after a short while that there was a huge gap between men who were Nice Guys and those who were Bad Boys.

In discussing this with a number of women, all of them agreed that men do not meld the Bad Boy with Mr. Nice Guy. Either they are decent men who don't know how to properly light their fire, or bad guy loser types who know how to excite a woman but behave badly in every other regard. When I offered that what they were seeking was a nice, decent, wonderful guy they could count on who knew how to be a bad boy in intimate situations, every one of them emphatically agreed. All of them indicated this was something they keenly desired in their initial encounters with a man, as well as ongoing through their relationship.

There are certainly many things lost in the translation from Venusian to Martian, but the aspect of how much a woman would love for her guy to be a bad boy is something that simply does not occur to most men. Forget the true bad boys, they are not redeemable.

But there is more than just capturing the attention and imagination of a beautiful, intelligent woman by combining the Bad Boy with the Good Guy. Yes, that is the foundation that is crucial to have, but going forward involves more. Having her want to be with you, and you only is simple, but not easy. For a very long time I have been with a beautiful and very accomplished woman. When people meet us, and I tell them about her, they wonder aloud 'what's she doing with you?' You will find out why in the pages that follow.

This book is for all those decent guys out there who are dying to know how to excite the women in their lives and willing to do whatever it takes to please them, make their self-confidence soar, and be the kind of all-encompassing male that a quality woman will want to be with for good. And, of course, all the women who obtained this book and handed it over to their guys, so they can get what they REALLY want – on an ongoing basis!

For Kris

The ultimate reward for being a Good Bad Boy

Jeff d'Avanzo

Chapter 1

The Good and Bad of Being Mr. Nice Guy

<u>Why nice guys finish last</u>

You're a nice guy; a decent guy. You were taught to respect women and you make every effort to do so. You show up on time; since being late is discourteous and sends a message to a woman that you're indifferent, or worse, don't really care about her. Politeness is something that you practice with a religious fervor, since being rude will never be well received by any woman. Inherently, you're very patient with the women in your life, knowing they are more sensitive than you and are subject to emotional highs and lows that are sometimes beyond their control. Aware of this, you understand these situations, almost to a fault. All in all, you've tried your hardest to become reliable, available and basically 'be there' when women have needed you.

So, why is it that when you try to move smoothly from being Mr. Nice Guy to engaging a woman on a more physical and sexual level, complete and utter failure is instead your companion every time?

Let's be fair, most men never had any kind of an effective sexual mentor in their formative years to provide the elusive Rosetta Stone of Women. Some had an evolved sister or mother sit down and try to explain what relating with girls would be all about. However, while this may sound ideal, masculinity, not fostered at least partly by a male mentor, will flounder. So will this man's efforts at engaging women in a confident manner.

Other unfortunate souls have suffered a time honored rite of passage--the oppressive 'birds and bees' talk with a Neanderthal Dad. Many times this talk trumpets the merits of being a 'man's man' and not to be too emotional or sensitive. Unfortunately, this could resurface years later in the form of emotional unavailability, lack of communication of feelings and other behavioral difficulties stemming from a general bewilderment on how to act around the female half of the population.

Worst of all is the 'classroom on the corner', where the collective sexual unconsciousness of the neighborhood boys conspire to thwart any possibility of evolving a young male's sensual awareness to any healthy degree. Here all the rumors, innuendo, myths and urban legends involving girls that have been gleaned from media stereotypes have significant sway. Music videos, television and film, soft and hardcore pornographic magazines and online websites and videos as well as other sources continue to foster an unrealistic standard of women's looks, appearance and sexuality. With this as a source of sexual education, it's easy to see where boys physically grow into men, yet often remain boys emotionally when it comes to dealing with their female counterparts.

Is there a cure for nice guy-itis?

The typical 21st century male must start the process of becoming a Good Bad Boy by first re-learning what interacting with a woman – as an adult – entails.

Let's focus on the destination. The goal is to become a Good Bad Boy, but what does that actually mean? A Good Bad Boy is someone who has the knowledge and confidence to be able to be the driving force in physical intimacy, yet be able to listen, understand and cater to any and all of his partner's wishes, needs and desires and still maintain his stature as an uncompromised male. Being a Good Bad Boy entails knowing when it is time to kiss a woman – or more – but more importantly know when it is time not to push the sexual agenda. Being a Good Bad Boy involves a comprehensive understanding of what a woman needs at any time, and given that in many instances the woman herself may not know what she wants, well, that makes for a daunting challenge. However, the rewards are more than worth the effort.

An important aspect is conviction. A Good Bad Boy needs to be able to lead when it's time to lead, provide a solution to a problem when it is required, yet also have the sense to know when to let things be – to know when less is more. Women desire a Good Bad Boy because they can cover so much territory, both physically and emotionally. It involves a higher lever of emotional maturity and confidence and the ability to lead. A Good Bad Boy is always ready with a plan or idea, and this way a woman can agree or change the plan to her liking. A Good Bad Boy is evolved enough to let a woman have her way since making a woman happy in her heart is his ultimate goal. Women want a man who can take charge – but is smart enough to never tell a woman what to do unless he is asked for his opinion. And even then he should think twice!

For example, I was shopping at the supermarket one evening after a tough day at work, and being the typical bachelor I was at the time, I was perusing the frozen food section to see what I could easily crank up for dinner that didn't involve too much work and even less cleanup. Out of the corner of my eye I noticed a very attractive woman a few yards down the aisle also looking at the frozen food case, likely for the same reasons as myself. Since an important goal is to always be thinking in Good Bad Boy mode, I deduced that she was trying to figure out her dinner situation for the evening, and it was highly likely she was dining by herself – if she was going to be dining with a boyfriend or husband she wouldn't be at the frozen food case. She was considering an easy meal for herself. This was an irresistible situation – a beautiful woman who didn't have her dinner plans set for the evening. A Good Bad Boy is always ready when Opportunity Knocks, and right now it was trying to kick down the door!

As we have just mentioned, conviction is very important and you will learn in the coming chapters how to embrace a wonderful occurrence like this and know how to act and what to say.

I walked up to the woman, and I figured that since we were in the same situation I would propose something that would be mutually beneficial, but also make it a very sexy invitation for adventure. I said to her " You know, it looks like both of us are trying to figure out our dinners, and it doesn't look like either of us are very happy about it. Let me propose an idea. Let's skip the frozen dinner nonsense and let me take you out to dinner. Right now, any restaurant you want to go to."

Of course she could have easily and politely refused, me being a stranger and offering a provocative invitation from completely out of the blue. However, the temptation of being offered a dinner of choice by a sexy, handsome stranger was too good for her to pass up, and she smiled back at me and took her cell phone and called a friend of hers who was a hostess at a restaurant to arrange a table right away.

Now, there are risks involved with a situation like this, some of them obvious, some less so. She could have refused, and while that would have been a disappointment, you'll learn later that a Good Bad Boy is only interested in a woman that is interested in him – and what he has to offer. For her, there are the obvious risks of going out with a complete and utter stranger, but she countered that by arranging to meet where a friend worked, so she had a safety net.

The other risk involved was that I offered her dinner at the restaurant of *her choice*, and in a major city that can be a very expensive invitation. However, a Good Bad Boy never goes back on what he says, and I would never have made the offer if I wasn't willing to cover it – regardless of place and cost. And believe me, I was tested. Her good friend was a hostess at one of Wolfgang Puck's restaurants and it would be an expensive night. If I backed out at this point, as many guys would have, I would have been a complete jerk and cheapskate and there is nothing sexy at all about either of those – I was creating a fantasy situation and needed to see it through. Good Bad Boys are always differentiating themselves from other guys and simply doing what you say you will do goes a long way! Besides, it would have been weeks if I wanted a reservation at this restaurant using my own devices, so she was already adding greatly to the evening.

Our dinner was delicious and fun, with a lot of sexy flirtation and getting to know each other. And boy did I get a special kiss good night after this evening! There were many risks involved with the invitation that I offered earlier in the evening, but as they say, the greater the risk, the greater the potential reward. I was greatly rewarded this night – yes by the obvious affection of a beautiful woman, but more being a Good Bad Boy and creating some very special moments that will last a very long time.

Being all things to all people is impossible, but becoming a Good Bad Boy covers a lot of ground when it comes to most women.

A woman wants to be treated fairly and respectfully, romanced properly but also desires to have a man romantically and sexually sweep her off her feet. She wants a guy that is safe, reliable, someone she can count on, yet knows when it's time to be a Bad Boy and ignite the flames of desire. A Nice Guy only sees half of all this, a Good Bad Boy has learned from experience and the women in his life how to bridge this difficult rift.

The first concept that must be stressed is for men to do a whole lot less thinking – particularly when it comes to what they think works with women. In place of all that wasted brain usage, we'll take a lesson from women, and trust intuition. So, bookmark this thought for later – *Feel More and Think Less*. If you learn nothing else but that, you'll still be miles ahead of the rest of the mob. Feel More. Think Less.

Let's make something clear from the onset. Being a Nice Guy is a very good thing. A very important thing. In fact, without being a Nice Guy, you will never get to venture into the garden of sensual delights that any self-respecting woman offers. The key is keeping Mr. Nice Guy in his proper place, and not let him handle the tasks that a Good Bad Boy should be responsible for. Where in the past you were baffled by how to hook the attentions of a cute female, you will learn when it's time for the Nice Guy to take a hike, and when to step in as a good seductive Bad Boy, and switch gears between the two effortlessly. For now, let's discuss and dissect Mr. Nice Guy, and make him play his role correctly.

Emotional Safety

While what you say to a woman is always important, it's a man's actions that will ultimately shape the relationship between the two of you. All of the attributes discussed at the beginning of the chapter, especially respect for a woman's feelings and opinions, are required for developing a woman's trust and her being able to confide in you.

The foremost task for Mr. Nice Guy is having his words and deeds reach a point of consistency that a woman feels emotionally safe with him. If a woman feels emotionally safe, then – with time, patience, effort and trust – her heart, mind, body and soul will be open and accessible. Many times the Nice Guy will spend time with a woman being nice and attentive, but all the time and effort is focused on a sexual payoff somewhere down the road. This mentality must always be avoided, it is a 'strings attached' attitude, and a complete waste of your time. It simply isn't nice, and women will view you as creepy – a term you *never* want associated with yourself. You're better off being dead than being a creep, and from a relationship standpoint, a creep is dead anyway.

So, if you can't do a favor for an attractive woman without expectation of *anything* in return, then don't do it at all. Good Bad Boys know that doing kind deeds across the board, without the anticipation of some sort of payoff, is the only route to Good Bad Boy Enlightenment. Besides, the real secret is that a truly kind individual who gives freely without want or expectation of anything in return is *much more likely* to get what he wants. I'm not talking Porsches and swimming pools; this is about engaging the women in your life on the level you've only dreamed of. The change comes from the inside; assuming you're now truly free of expectation, you don't feel a lack or loss because nothing has happened. You've done a selfless, kind act and asked or expected nothing in return. You feel better, and it reflects to others around you. Women pick up on it, and they are more attracted to you. They *love* guys with this attitude. Do kind and selfless deeds without any expectation. Doing them anonymously is even better; it's a higher evolution of this belief. Remember, it's about how you feel on the inside, and this will make you feel better about yourself all around.

    I was recently in a store where an attractive mother was struggling to do her shopping and keep her son in control. While trying to amuse her child, some items dropped from her possession and without any thought, I stepped over to her and picked them up. She gave me the standard thank you, but being a Good Bad Boy, I'm always looking for opportunities to practice my craft. I looked at the toy, and commented "That's really for you, isn't it?" Of course, it wasn't, but the point is, on top of the nice deed, I connected on another level, and made her smile and brought a moment of warmth. Most importantly, this had nothing to do with trying to engage her sexually – it was a fun moment with only a hint of flirtation, and we both went our separate ways and got on with our lives. If you practice the attitude of giving without expectation, you will make great gains in your relations with   women.

The importance of this goes back to a woman's emotional safety. If she knows you're doing things for her without any expectation from it, she will trust you more easily and desire being closer to you, whether or not that manifests in any physical activity. Although, be assured that if there is any kissing, or more, that's going to happen, it will only be if she reaches this comfort level with you.

The Platonic Friendship Trap

One big dilemma Nice Guys usually face is getting lost on the Road to Platonic Friendship far too late for them to get back in the right direction. As stated earlier, there's nothing wrong with acts of kindness without expectation of recompense. However, if your initial efforts at trying to gain the favors of a fair maiden involve fixing broken items, carrying heavy objects, killing vermin, and so on, you're essentially saying to her PLATONIC FRIEND – DO NOT TOUCH. Again, this is assuming that she doesn't have a big initial attraction to you. The only sure way to know that a woman is attracted to you is that it's been communicated to you in a direct manner--"Hey, she was smiling at me, and looking me in the eyes...a lot!" Anything short of this shall be interpreted as Friends Only!

Be conscious of your initial interactions. The early involvement here is a task oriented one having nothing to do with romance, so the platonic course has been set. Don't blame any woman later for leading you on or taking advantage of you if you get things started in this direction. Any woman can find a handyman in the Yellow Pages, finding a guy that can sweep her off her feet and take her breath away is a little more challenging. Essentially, by sending out the message that you're a nice guy and that you're willing to do favors for a woman, they will be more than happy to oblige your wishes. You've communicated to her that it's fine to take that course. Women are quite sharp, but they can't read your mind. By failing to effectively communicate your wishes you've now dug yourself into the Platonic Grave, and rest assured, there is little hope of ever getting out of it.

The problem here is that Mr. Nice Guy has taken the lead role. He has his place, and it's an important one, but on the journey to being a Good Bad Boy, it is essential for a man to know when it is time to be nice and when it's time to be 'bad'. They are to co-exist, dependent on each other, but like a good team, will not interfere with the other's area of expertise. Those defined areas will become clearer later on. For now, its time to learn more about women.

<u>Being Good, Being Bad and What Women Really Want</u>

What a woman really wants in a man can be written about and discussed from now until the end of time, but our focus is on one particular aspect within this subject. If you know this fact, and then learn how to become adept within it, I can assure you the women in your life will be very happy, and therefore you will be as well. And what is this great kernel of sensual knowledge? *Most women want Mr. Nice Guy to know how to look and act like a Bad Boy.* They want a man who knows when its time to act like a gentleman and then knows when its time to be anything but. And yes, this generally means sensually and sexually.

Sure women desire a Bad Boy, but that hardly means they want a Loser in their lives, which most Bad Boys are. While women want the guy they're involved with to possess the characteristics of the sensitive, well-mannered good guy, those traits usually appeal to their common sense, and are not what sends their hearts and libidos racing. You have to satisfy both the heart and the mind!

In trying to figure out your way to what a woman is really looking for, you should spend a few moments getting educated on the kinds of men they should be *avoiding at all costs*. While it may seems like common sense that a decent fellow as yourself would never purposely engage in the following behavior patterns, being aware of them serves a couple of purposes. Firstly, you'll be more sensitive to the kinds of truly bad guys there are out there that women are subjected to, and how you can set yourself apart from them. Secondly, for all the women that are looking in, here's a good reminder of the kind of *real* Bad Boys that, if you want to have a healthy and happy personal life, you will never let get anywhere close to you.

Here's a summary of Real Bad Boys:

- *The Narcissist* is a personality type weaved so well into the relationship landscape that there are several sub categories of narcissism that have to be considered.

And just a heads up--there are plenty of women narcissists that this will apply to as well!

- *The Sexual Narcissist* is a predator that encourages deviant sexual behavior and will lure you in by encouraging and approving 'open-mindedness'. This person will use guilt to manipulate you into uncomfortable actions.

- *The Violent Narcissist*--the name says it all. The 'world is against me' and will sabotage relationships by harassment and provocation. Also will try to make you look like the 'out of control' person. Very dangerous as using physical violence is a means to an end with this person.

- *The Paranoid Narcissist* is suspicious of everything and accuses you of many things without justification. Avoids exposure and will use you to hide from facing realities.

- *The Preaching Narcissist* accuses others of failing unrealistically high standards of honesty and integrity while secretly lying and cheating behind your back. Full of false moral integrity and high minded – all to deflect from their utter lack of character.

- *The Forewarning Narcissist* will actually tell you up front what a bad person they are but is banking on your thinking you can change them--that you falling for the ruse that because this person has been 'up front and honest' you can trust them. Then when you are devastated by their bad behavior they play the 'I told you who I was when you met me' defense. Next time one of these folks lets you know that they are no good and you shouldn't be around them--confound their plan by actually believing them and running away at top speed

- *The Finger Pointing Narcissist* will blame you and others for all failures and will never accept any responsibility. This person projects everything onto others and uses their 'forgiveness' as their hook.

- *The Contrite Narcissist* will admit to their bad behavior and promises to change while asking forgiveness for their transgressions. This person is counting on your hitting the reset button so they can start the whole cycle over again. This person promises to change but never does.

In addition to the Festival of Narcissists, also be aware of these other special folks:

- *The Manipulator* pits people against each other and relies heavily on disinformation. Intent on controlling others, and is very skilled at keeping friends and potential victims apart from each other. Charming and charismatic, is a master with using words to gain their objective which is usually financial. Politicians and television evangelists fall into this category.

- *The Substance Abuser* is once again all in the name. Overindulgence in sex, drugs, alcohol, food or whatever will fill the endless void for self gratification. This person will try to coerce you into joining the draining whirlpool of excess.

- *The Gambler* is a foolhardy risk taker putting himself and all those around him in jeopardy. Never learns from mistakes and has no remorse about continually causing ruin from poor impulsive decision making. Keep your finances as far away as possible.

- *The Soul Mate* is a nefarious and crafty type that preys on those that will respond to their button pushing. Hits you like gangbusters, sweeps you off your feet doing and saying all the right things and has all the same interests and tastes that you do. It's all a ruse, as those interests are a mirror to deflect from this person's lack of depth and false integrity. The only objective is garnering your attention whether it's good or bad. This person appears too good to be true and that's because it is. Very insidious and hard to detect, anyone who seems too perfect warrants deeper examination.

Once again, by gaining knowledge on how real Bad Boys operate, you have the opportunity to achieve one of the Good Bad Boy's primary objectives, which is to separate yourself from the rest of the clueless male populace.

<u>Bad is Good and Good is Bad?</u>

Women desire both the Nice Guy and the Bad Boy in the same package. Many men scratch their heads and don't understand how they can want both a bad and a good guy. Think of it as a Volkswagen Golf with a Ferrari Engine in it – practical, roomy and reliable but can send the adrenaline racing in less than 6 seconds. The important thing to know is that they are looking for the Bad Boy only in the physical realm or those areas of their psyche that stimulate the physical. They want the Bad Boy in a sexual context, because this guy turns them on – the outlaw, the rebel, and the guy who doesn't follow the rules and does things his own way. Someone who presents an element of danger and risk that is many times thrilling to a woman. However, bringing this mythic figure into the reality of dating is challenging, to say the least. Women don't *really* want a dangerous guy in their lives, since physical safety is at the top of a woman's priority list. Misbehaving Bad Boys that do not pick up the phone and call or display any other actions that show that a woman is valued and desired will always lead to misery. It is very important to know the difference between a Bad Boy and a

Good Bad Boy. One will always by adored by women and the other will always cause heartbreak to them. Its obvious which one you want to be.

Women want to have a nice guy in their lives. A fellow that they can rely on--shows up on time, calls regularly, listens, brings flowers, is caring and so on. However, here's what most guys never figure out- Mr. Nice Guy generally doesn't get a woman hot and bothered. He's important to a woman everywhere except the bedroom. And we all know what an important room the bedroom is.

I once was out on a first date with a woman, who was a very attractive college professor, and we had a very good time at our meal and flirting, and it was clear there was a mutual attraction. After our dinner we went for a walk around the neighborhood, which was a trendy area with shops and other restaurants. While we were walking and talking, I was looking for the right place and time to raise the stakes. We turned a corner and there was a long wall, and I stopped, and then she stopped as well. I then put my hand on her abdomen and gently pushed her up against the wall, and stepped closer to her. She then looked at me and said, somewhat breathlessly, "Oh, you're a Bad Boy, aren't you?" I said nothing, as that would have taken away from the moment, but those were special words to any Good Bad Boy. I gave her a deep, long and very substantial kiss that answered her question in the most affirmative manner possible. How you get to this point of knowledge and confidence will be shown later, but the point is, Mr. Nice Guy took her to dinner, and then stepped away at the appropriate time to let the Good Bad Boy take over and do his magic.

> ### Good Bad Boy Tip #1
>
> *Most women agree that men do not meld the Bad Boy with Mr. Nice Guy. Most men are either one or the other, which leaves women with a frustrating choice. Either they are decent men who don't know how to properly light their fire, or bad guy loser types who know how to excite a woman but behave badly in every other regard. Start viewing yourself in a different light in your encounters with women – you will now be a driving force to your goals instead of passively waiting for what crumbs that may fall your way.*

One large mistake that many men make is incorrectly focusing on what they think an ideal woman is in terms of behavior, looks, or actions. Since virtually every man doesn't come close to getting this right, it's a good idea to examine what exactly men are seeking in the relationship arena.

What Do Men Really Want?

Ask any man what it is that he is seeking when dating the opposite sex and you will encounter a range of answers that will stretch from the sublime to the ridiculous, with the majority leaning towards the latter. The infamous "I'll know it when I see/hear/smell/feel/taste it" can be generally translated as "I have no idea at all what I really want". Often, men rely on what their minds (read: eyes) tell them instead of their hearts, and often make poor choices as far as dates are concerned. Men will be all over the place as far as what they want, desiring someone who is attractive, sexy, smart, salacious, a good cook, listens well, is a caretaker, nurturer, great map reader, and so on. The list gets even more specific in places like New York, Paris, Rome or Los Angeles where there are a plethora of pretty women; the premium on attractiveness goes up significantly.

To complicate things further, some men will look to their mothers as the source of what they desire in a woman. More accurately, if their maternal relationship was a healthy one, men will many times try to seek the same characteristics. Likewise, if the relationship was not very good, men will gravitate away from those characteristics.

While utilizing familiarity with a parent as a guide for connecting with the opposite sex is understandable, it is not what we are seeking here. Being a Good Bad Boy means working from within, and in order to accomplish this, a clear roadmap on what characteristics in another are being sought is completely necessary.

It's easy to say this, but doing it is a whole other matter. Most men have a better shot with quantum physics problems or plumbing repair than they do with defining their ideal woman. However, it need not be so hard. It's very important to have an awareness of the characteristics you desire in a woman *from the beginning*. The sooner you know the level of mutual compatibility, the sooner you know the proper path to follow, which will lead to your destination instead of wandering around lost in the dating desert. Being clear on who you desire not only makes your life much simpler, women will sense that clarity in you and will find it attractive. While most men look outside themselves for the answer here, once again we'll take the path of Bad Boy Enlightenment and look within.

In seeking a compatible companion, it can be simple. Start by thinking about the things--aspects, habits, ideologies, and so on that are important to you, and list them. Then ponder the importance of these in a woman you'd like to date. Here are a few areas to consider to get started:

- Intelligence--When it comes to a woman that you've just met and are trying to know better, it seems that there is far more time focused on what's going on from the neck down instead of what exists between her ears. You may not need a woman to have a doctorate, but you should be honest with yourself if you're going to feel intimidated by her if she's very accomplished. There should be an inner ease here on both sides, without anyone having to prove anything. Be yourself and see if the minds mesh. This is a very important, usually overlooked area, and many times the level of intellect goes hand in hand with level of imagination, experimentation, creativity, adventure and so on. For better or worse, there is a vast range of intellect out there, and if your witty humor is not being appreciated, or you find your potential lover having to define words you've not heard before – assuming you're comfortable enough with yourself to admit to her you don't know the meaning – red flags should begin to fly.

- Looks – Need more be said? This one is in the eye of the beholder. Sure, it matters, but remember, it isn't everything. Sometimes beauty can blind you to characteristics that are far less pretty. Attractiveness is more than looks, and someone who is truly beautiful is that way below the surface – sexiness is a state of mind and displayed in attitude and demeanor. These are facts all Good Bad Boys know instinctively.

- Profession – What a woman does for a living will be of importance, because there is a wide range of different professions and responsibilities, and that means a wide range of characteristics to fulfill them. A woman who is in administrative positions may likely have a very different personality than that of someone who is an executive, and consequently a more accomplished woman, at least in the professional sense, will many times be a stronger personality and more independent. While men often claim that they desire an independent, professionally accomplished woman, once they become involved, they then have great difficulty with her commitment to her work and busy schedule, her unavailability, and complain how they are not getting the attention they want. You can't have it both ways, so be clear on what your preferences are in this area, otherwise everyone will end up highly unsatisfied.

- Political /Ideological – Maybe it doesn't matter to you that you're conservative and someone you're dating is liberal. Maybe it does, but considering it and what it means could be important. A difference in political leanings doesn't have to effect a connection between you and a woman unless you choose to let it be an issue. If there is enough common ground on other ideologies that can be used as a bridge to join the two of you as opposed to focusing on one single aspect and using that as a wall. Of course, in simple dating, a subject area such as this one is less important than chemistry, but you probably would want to know if you're trying to seduce a member of some extremely left or right wing organization so you could act accordingly, such as taking the first opportunity to make a speedy exit – unless of course you happen to *also* belong to that extreme faction as well, and then you'll have plenty to talk about!

- Activities – Someone who shares an interest in doing the same things you do--hiking, sailing, motorcycling, road trips, playing or watching sports, and so on. If you're an outdoors person that loves to camp and hike in the mountains, and your new date's idea of camping is staying at the Marriott instead of the Hilton – that's right, red flags fly again.

There are dozens more categories, but at this point it's important you are clear on whom you are seeking. If you jumped in your car in Boston and wanted to take a drive to Springfield, it would seem a straight shot down the Massachusetts Turnpike is in order. However, that's assuming you're going to *that* Springfield. You may, in fact, really want to travel to the one in Ohio or Illinois or even Missouri. In each case, you're going to have to know exactly where you're going because each of them ultimately involves taking a different route, and some taking longer than others.

A lot of time will be saved and headaches avoided if you know what you want. By being clear in this regard you will recognize much more quickly those who you are compatible with and those you are not. Bear is mind, that as fabulous as you think you might be, you're not everyone's cup of tea, and vice versa. If you recognize and acknowledge that early on, and part ways gracefully, it's always an action that is taking care of yourself.

Of course, you may be concerned that in being much more clear and specific on whom you want to date, you're going to exclude all the other women that don't fit the desired profile and have far less women to potentially date. Or you're interfering with what the fates may have in store for you. You're welcome to turn over your love life to a cosmic roll of the dice and a bazillion to one chance that you'll encounter your female alter ego while you're at the market. If you have that kind of time, patience and faith, kudos for you. For the rest of us pragmatic mortals, here's a thought. Say there are 500 single women in your city in your desired age range. Now, let's assume you are very, very clear on what type of characteristics and attributes you are seeking from this group, and that will eliminate 99% of them. Of course, most men will wail like a soiled infant when they here that percentage--but wait crybaby! That still leaves five women that meet your very precise, very specific criteria. And while five may not seem a big number like 500, you will be hard pressed to date five women in any kind of short time frame, and still have your normal life. It's about someone who fits your parameters, and you only need one. There's a decent chance within that number there is someone who really rings your bell.

Good Bad Boy Tip #2

By being clear what you desire you maintain your way on the path of Bad Boy Enlightenment and by going from your inside out to the rest of the dating world, you maintain your stature and power. You have given yourself clarity on the type of woman you would like to pursue – stick to it. Stay true to yourself and put that out to the world. Many women will respond to it, but remember to Think Less and Feel More on what comes back to you.

A friend of mine who was dating online posted a profile that he figured would not be of interest to 99.9% of the women who happened to look at it. Sounds like a bad plan but it really made sense. You're not trying to serial date; your goal is to find that woman that you have good chemistry with. He was very clear on what he was looking for, but he didn't make the mistake of spelling out a list of what he was seeking in a woman. That is a terrible plan of action for dating and will turn most women off – just avoid it. Instead he was very comfortable with who he is and wrote a profile that he intended to appeal to the most creative and adventurous women out there – he was really target marketing! He was trying to clear the room of all those women he knew he would not be interested in and focused on the much smaller number that he would want to connect with. From there he could see from the few responses which woman really was the best fit to what he was seeking, and proceeded ahead. It worked brilliantly because he found a wonderful companion who shares many things in common with him and they've been happily married for quite a long time now.

However, at this point I would be remiss to allow you to unleash this newly charged male fury on an unsuspecting female population half-cocked, so to speak.

Why, you may ask? Well, one assumes that the main reason why this book interests you is that you're dying to figure out what it is that women really want – at least in the specific regard covered in these chapters. You now have more clarity on the kind of woman you are seeking out, instead of just hanging around at a club or party and reacting to whichever woman happens to respond to your ill-informed advances. However, you're only part way to your desired destination. You may be clear on where you're heading, but you have no clue what to do once you get there. You need to develop a Good Bad Boy understanding of women.

Think of it this way. You are embarking on a photo safari in Africa, and you've decided to pursue only elephants instead of lions. The clarity of choice is laudable, but you still have little understanding of how to do it without local assistance. Sure, you know what they look like and they travel in herds, and eat a lot of vegetation, have to drink fifty gallons of water a day (well, maybe you didn't know *that*), but you have no idea of where they roam, when and why or any of their other behavioral traits. From your perspective right now women are wild animals – beautiful, wonderful to gaze upon, but dangerous to approach in any manner lest you get your heart or ego trampled. You wouldn't just walk up to an elephant in the wild and start snapping flash photos, unless you're capable of running at world-class speed. Hence, a new understanding of women needs to wash over you in a flash flood manner – quickly and completely.

Once you have a better understanding of women, you will have much better instincts on timing, what to say, what to do and what is too much or not enough, and a thousand other things. It's not so much acquiring an encyclopedic knowledge of women; that would take thousands of pages and more time than any of us could possibly spend on the subject, enticing as it may be. You'll just get to a place of knowing what you need to know and the rest will fall into place. The first order of business is that an understanding of a very different way of viewing the world is in order.

Time to take a very deep breath and step into the remarkable, quizzical and beautiful parallel universe where women exist.

Chapter 2

Understanding Venusian

For centuries men have been wracking their brains trying to understand women, and the total of the energy exerted on this topic would provide enough power to keep Cincinnati well lit for a few years. Nowhere does our Good Bad Boy Mantra of *Think Less and Feel More* apply than on the perilous topic of understanding women. So, initially we'll just have to purge all those previous notions of women that are now clouding your mind out into the air, where they will hopefully vaporize and not cause too much of a smog cloud.

Oscar Wilde, as with many other subjects, summed up his view on women in a single phrase. He wrote, "Women are meant to be loved, not understood", and the truth of this should not be underestimated. It's probably not so ironic that a brilliant gay man was able to enlighten the rest of the male masses on how to handle the matter of relating with women. However, just parroting his well-chosen words will hardly gain you insight on the female half of the species. Deeper examination is necessary before you can put into action this newly acquired knowledge and think less. It does sound contrary, but remember, we're on a female planet now, and the frequency of conflicting concepts will multiply at an alarming rate.

You Think Too Much

One exasperating trait of men many women dislike is the general tendency to survey problems and then go about solving them in their own unique way. It could be that this is wired into the male DNA from the hunter/gatherer days, but some of the modern day consequences of this characteristic are poorly done home repair projects, lack of foresight in financial and retirement planning, and a complete aversion to road maps among many other unattractive traits. The most egregious of these, however, is the male attribute that imagines that he has a new and brilliant insight to the way a woman may be running her life. While this is perfectly acceptable, arguably gallant, when it is requested of them, much more often than not these pearls of wisdom are ushered forth without any form of invitation. Women are very accomplished and have gotten quite far without the sage advice of a male on how to go about their business. Suffice it to say, the worst kind of advice is that of the unsolicited variety. Add to that the fact that most men don't have a very good grasp of women anyway, and then you have some really useless information being foisted upon a soon-to-be angry member of the female half of the population. Let's proceed and find out how to love women, and by not trying to figure them out, leaving everyone much happier.

Men, in their charmingly simplistic view, assume that if a woman wants him to take the lead that is a comprehensive invitation to advise and instruct on all matters and decisions in a woman's life. Nothing could be further from the truth. A trip to the dance floor may assist us in clarifying this line of thought.

Many women love to dance, and many men, straight men that is, really aren't that keen on it. By dance, I mean real dancing, like salsa, ballroom or swing, with prescribed steps that are followed to a considerable degree. What I'm not referring to is white boys flailing around on the dance club floor, looking as if a horde of fire ants have been dropped into their pants.

Lets imagine a man taking a woman to the dance floor, and as they proceed, he tells her at every step and move what she should do, where to go, how he thinks she should move there, even though she is already skilled in the dance steps. This will quickly become a miserable experience for the woman, who would not be questioned for kicking this man in the groin for such actions. A woman would be understandably quite angry with this behavior, and at the time she storms off, this man would think, in a frustrated manner, "But she said she wanted me to lead!"

Now consider the same man taking a woman onto the dance floor, leading her through the dance. He leads her as far as the structure of the dance with the music is concerned; he has his steps, and she has hers that juxtaposes with his. It is a balanced equation, a symmetry that flows naturally, and no words need be spoken to have it be so. A man, in this specific relationship, provides the blank canvas for the woman to fill with colors and definition. A man allows the space for the woman to fill with her style, manner and grace. It is lovely and sexy, and all of it done as a partnership.

Good Bad Boy Tip #3

The crucial difference is that lead does not mean control, and it is vitally important for any man to understand this distinction if he is to attain Good Bad Boy status. Many women will state that they love a man who 'takes charge' or 'takes control', but these phrases refer to very specific situations, like knowing when to firmly take a woman and kiss her for the first, or hundredth time. Taking charge doesn't signify taking over. Women really enjoy it when men plan an evening out at a romantic restaurant, but that doesn't mean he should tell her what she should eat. Become conscious right now of the difference between leading and controlling – it's a hugely important point to understand.

So, it's essential for a Good Bad Boy to know how to lead without taking control, and that's only one of many conundrums that a guy will face with women. So, of course, you defer to Mr. Wilde's infinite wisdom and forego trying to figure them out. What a Good Bad Boy will concern himself with is being an irresistible guy, and we'll develop that later. For now, we'll concentrate on successfully interacting with women, and once again, that means thinking a whole lot less.

Barring any serious psychological issues on your part, you're probably like a lot of the Nice Guys out there in that pleasuring a woman is important to you, and doing it well is a priority. This has to be one of your main goals to have any hope of being truly adored by women. Good Bad Boys have a quiet sense of pride in knowing that they are skillful lovers, and enjoy bringing a woman as much pleasure as she can handle. In the arena of being an adroit seducer and love maker, they already know the secrets and keep it to themselves. Good Bad Boys don't brag about their sexual activities, they've already been told by the women in their lives how special they are, and their opinions matter the most to them. Hopefully you are already aware that you *never* boast about your past sexual experiences to a woman, unless never having sex with her is a goal for you. Even if she asks you about it, assume a self-effacing attitude and politely side step any specific mention of your experiences. If you're a skilled lover, she already knows you've been around the block a number of times. Her *imagining* that you've been with a lot of women will potentially turn her on, thinking you're a lovely, naughty Bad Boy, and now she's captured your attentions all to herself. You *telling* her you've been with a bunch of other girls will completely kill the illusion she's created in her mind, make her feel diminished and unexceptional, as well as taking away her fantasy guy. Now you're just another player who has completely turned her off. Let her run with the imagery and keep your mouth shut.

<u>Two Ears versus One Mouth</u>

It is now time to discuss the most important step down the Path of Bad Boy Enlightenment. You should etch this permanently into your brain as soon as possible, that if you really want to become a Good Bad Boy; you have to learn how to *Listen To Women*.

Listening to other guys when you were a boy got you off on the wrong foot, and now its time to set you back in the right direction. If you learn nothing else, please learn how to listen to women. What this entails is not only *listening*, but *hearing* them as well. Yes, another nuance for you to comprehend and excel at right away. So many times women have expressed how men don't listen to them. Good Bad Boys have no interest in being like the unenlightened hordes of other men out there, so they take the extra time to become great listeners. Hear a woman out, offer support or and when it is requested--and only then--offer an opinion on the topic of conversation. If a woman is confiding to you about herself and that familiar male urge to give your opinion starts to come over you, do everything within your power to stifle it. Bite your tongue, smile politely, think about baseball, nod your head, excuse yourself to the bathroom so you can regain composure and remind yourself not to think. Do everything you can to kill this impulse. If you lose this regrettable tendency, you will automatically become much more attractive to women. You're acknowledging their words and thoughts and giving them weight and consideration. Really listening to a woman is something they're not used to from most men, so it will set you apart, and make you more special to them.

Now that you've managed to corral this lousy instinct, we're going to turn it completely around. Staying with the theme of paradoxes, you are now going to do something that fights every drop of testosterone that is coursing through that male vessel of yours. You are now going to *Ask Questions*.

One commonality to all Good Bad Boys is that they seek and recognize opportunities to unlock the doors that separate men from women. This is absolutely one of those occasions, and you must use it wisely. From my own experience and speaking to other Good Bad Boys, the way we became comfortable with women was by taking the time to listen and then ask questions, which cultivated our understanding of them. Show a genuine interest in what she is saying, and try to ask questions that reflect that. Being a male, you're more focused on what's going on below her neck than above, but if you really show concern about the travails of her cat--and mean it--she'll end up in your arms sooner anyway. Besides, you'll be out of your own head and exploring her world, and that will attract you to her, and vice versa, in a more meaningful and powerful way than left to your own primal devices.

This is all terrific, but how does one actually do this? Well, with anything else, the more you practice the better you get at it. However, you still have to start somewhere, and here's a suggestion. The next time you're having a conversation with a woman and are trying to practice Good Bad Boy techniques, listen carefully and follow her lead. If she's complaining about work, be sympathetic and agree with her about what a lousy boss she has, how unfair the work load is, how her company doesn't realize what a prize employee they have on their hands, and so on. Of course, this shouldn't be just lip service; you should listen to her and mean it! A woman will sense insincerity and then you'll really be in trouble. The important aspect to realize is that you need restraint, however, this does not give you license to use lame monosyllabic responses like 'Gee', 'Huh' 'Wow" or 'Sure'. A few caring comments as the discussion flows will ease things. Let her run with the conversation and get to know her.

Don't underestimate how important compassion is. A decent, evolved woman will value compassion and kindness greatly, and showing that you genuinely care about her will make you irresistible. Of course, women are far more complex than we males, so it's going to take much more than that to garner their complete adoration.

Up to this point, you've only been lobbing back verbal volleys in regard to her particular dilemma *du jour*. There are two types of questions you can now ask, each from different sides of the brain. You can ask nuts and bolts questions, like 'Why didn't your boss speak to you about the reorganization?' or other male-type questions that essentially ask 'What do you *think* about that?' The other more provocative and difficult, yet ultimately rewarding choice is to ask her 'How does that make you *feel*?'

This line of questioning and thinking is much more in the realm of the female, so you may get a protracted response. Stay focused, keep listening and offer support here and there, but don't overdo it. Once again, don't think too much, relax and simply have a conversation with this other person. Remember, a woman often times simply wants to know you're listening and that you care. If she wants you to solve the problem for her, she will ask you directly to do it.

While women have their similarities, Good Bad Boys already know that women are snowflakes, each one of them unique; physically, mentally and emotionally. Listen to each woman as if it's the first time you've listened to any woman, and never bring past assumptions or experiences to the table. In asking a woman how she feels, you become a student, so take the frame of mind that you're learning. The favorite subject of all Good Bad Boys is women, and they can *never* learn enough. Every Good Bad Boy is always a student and he never assumes he knows everything about women. That would be arrogant and egotistical, and this attitude will clear the room of all of the women you desire. If you disagree, you're welcome to try it your way. I'm confident you'll hate the results.

The objective is to become an accomplished listener, which is the other half of being a good communicator. If you only talk and don't listen, you're a blowhard, no matter how clever your words are. Listening leads to knowing the person you're communicating with, and knowing each other is vital to mutual attraction. You may be in conversation with a supermodel, but if she starts talking about how the minorities in her part of town have become intolerable, your attraction to this person should melt as quickly as ice dropped onto the backyard barbeque.

You're now listening attentively and occasionally putting in a *genuine* comment or question, and you connect with what this woman is saying and the attraction is growing. There is a caveat, however. Since this level of conversation and getting to know each other is not a one-way street, be ready to have the spotlight turned onto you. Asking her questions may seem difficult, but it pales in comparison to the terrifying moment when she asks 'How does that make *you* feel?'

<u>Authentic Communication</u>

Although this question is usually met by males with a head scratching response, there is a big incentive to respond to it in as honest and indisputable manner possible. This is another Big Truth that you need to recognize, memorize and never, ever forget--One of the main desires of women is being with a man who can *effectively share how he feels*. Being students in the art of women, Good Bad Boys are well aware of how important it is to females that a man be willing and able to successfully communicate his feelings. A man who is in touch with how he feels and then shares that with a woman will gain her heart much more quickly than if he doesn't want to be bothered with communicating them.

Try to remember to not give responses that tell her what you *think*, which is what most men will do. I'm no different since I tend to say what I think, but when asked how I feel about something I try to take a long moment before responding and think of certain buzzwords--angry, happy, sad, lonely, irritated, depressed, contented, lost--emotional words, words that for most men might as well be in Latin. I try to respond through whichever of those words come closest to how I'm feeling. This is a crucial time to remember the Good Bad Boy mantra--Think Less and Feel More. You can say that you're sad, elaborate a little on why, and not say much more than that. There is no need to justify or defend your feelings, they are not right or wrong, they are simply your feelings and they are legitimate. Women don't have to have it explained to them, they already understand. If you delve into another person's feelings, be willing to have yours examined as well. Handle this, and you'll have moved along nicely in your Good Bad Boy evolvement.

The intent of all this careful listening and sharing of feelings is the gaining access to the most treasured possession of a woman-- her *Trust*. Gaining trust is about you having integrity, and that integrity is built on your words and your actions. It is possible for you to bed a woman without her complete trust, if that is all you truly seek. However, you will miss the real riches that women will offer, and more importantly, you will never be a Good Bad Boy. Without trust you will never gain a foothold in a woman's heart, hence she will never adore you. Sure, she may think you're hot, but that's what she thinks, not how she feels. Good Bad Boys will never settle for just this, they know the value of being held precious in a woman's heart and attaining a permanent place there that belongs only to them. Building trust is the surest way to get there.

Here's a thought to consider – *Building trust is simple, but it is not easy.* Again, another paradox. Building trust *is* simple--you need only be honest, open, communicative, kind and consistent. However, when you add patience, understanding you'll have to do all this over an extended period of time, and then it becomes more challenging.

Good Bad Boy Tip #4

Always bear in mind that trust is <u>earned</u> and you can spend years building it but lose it all in a clueless moment. Building trust is a process you can control only in respect to your actions, which especially includes what you say. This is where Mr. Nice Guy is in order – follow his lead in terms of being respectful and kind. One of the biggest goals here is that when in the company of a woman, your words, deeds and action are that of a confident, poised MAN. Say what you mean and mean what you say!

When the Good Bad Boy and Mr. Nice Guy are put side by side and interact in the proper manner, leading with their strengths, then we have the type of man that we want to become, and the man that many, many women really desire. This is a vital notion, because in regard to trust, a woman will be more than happy to play with a sexy boy, but she will only surrender her heart and soul--and trust-- to a man who is genuine and authentic.

This real man is passionate. In olden tales he was valiant and easily faced danger. His heart is that of a lion, strong, wild yet loyal to those close to him. The daring, dashing, swashbuckling guy that maybe doesn't have it all figured out, but knew where he stood with women because he understood and loved them. Women yearn for this man and want to be swept away by him. Gain a woman's trust and you've taken a giant step towards becoming this man. This is the type of man that many of them will turn themselves over to willingly once that precious trust is gained. It is an effort that all Good Bad Boys make and persevere through until they reach this goal, knowing how crucial it is in relation to everything that follows after it. Now that the importance of acquiring a woman's deep trust is understood, it is time to move on to the next area in our probing of the female consciousness.

It is now time to venture further into territory that will baffle most males, but be assured, gaining understanding of it will significantly increase your attractiveness to women. We're now going to examine how to access your *feminine side.*

We've already touched on one of the basic foundations of accessing the feminine side, that being the ability to effectively express your feelings. Too often men have been taught that expressing their feelings is a sign of weakness, and this is quite unfortunate. Nothing could be further from the truth, at least from the view of women that I've known. Although sometimes it was not easy for me, the times where I was able to communicate through deep sadness or high elation how I felt to a woman, it helped forge a very strong emotional bridge between us. Take the following to heart, so to speak – effectively showing and expressing how you feel is a sign of strength, not weakness. A real man will cry without hesitation when truly sad, and laugh until he can't breathe when overcome with joy. Boys don't show how they feel; men are comfortable with their feelings and know the importance and significance of them. This is accessing your feminine side, and women will instinctively be drawn to you because of it.

The next important principal in harmonizing your masculine and feminine sides is learning about the balance between giving and receiving. On the surface, giving and receiving seems simple enough, but be assured that it is quite challenging. This is a highly important area as far as being clear on the inside and then translating those feelings and instincts into actions that go out into the world around you. Again – Think Less and Feel More.

Step back and take a look at the outside world for a moment. The ultimate authority in Nature is balance. The size of a herd of animals is balanced against what the land can provide it and the predators that hunt it. If any of these elements goes out of balance, the other elements are thrown off as well. If there is not enough food for a herd off the land, the herd suffers loss and the predators have less for their own and they suffer as well. If there is a lack of hunters, the herd gets too numerous, and the land cannot support them, suffers overuse and the herd overpopulates and can't sustain itself. Striking a balance allows for equilibrium between you and other women; an essential balance that has many layers. Being able to effectively receive as well as give without condition is vitally important.

The Circle of Giving and Receiving

Any good relationship, whether it is a new, sexually charged casual encounter or a marriage of many years, requires a level of balance to exist over time. Giving and receiving is a key component of this balance. Any relationship where one of the parties gets far more attention than the other or is spending much more time tending to the needs of the other is unbalanced, dysfunctional and unhealthy. This is not to say that things should be equal every minute of every day, since people tend to sometimes be more inclined to give than receive and vice versa. However, over time, things should generally equal out, at least to acceptable levels for the man and the woman.

Now, let's make some distinctions. There is a big difference between receiving and *taking*, and the difference is in the perception, actions and attitude of the recipient. Receiving involves recognition, gratitude, appreciation, kindness and consideration in regard to the other person's efforts. Taking is simply emotional theft – seizing what that other person offers to you with little or no thought of thanks or appreciation. It's obvious that taking is unkind and heartless, and those are characteristics that Good Bad Boys never associate themselves with. In a balanced equation between people, there will be a comparable level of giving and receiving. Allowing a more feminine side to emerge involves being able to effectively give and receive.

On the other side, giving has a number of dimensions. We discussed in the previous chapter the importance of doing kind deeds without expectation of anything in return. The same goes for giving. Giving should be done unconditionally, simply because the act itself is one that makes you feel better, and consequently, makes the woman you're involved with feel better as well. Giving, in the Good Bad Boy's thinking, is an extension of how he feels about the woman he's involved with. It's an opportunity to manifest through actions the emotions that are there, and it is a very powerful form of expression.

Although it is an impossible feat for most men to thoroughly understand women, one aspect of them that is required knowledge is that women are for the most part nurturers. This means they are natural givers, and do so in a manner that is not about control, it's just the way women are wired. Being able to receive from them unconditionally is essential in maintaining a natural balance. More importantly, it is a guy's responsibility to give back to a woman to help balance the giving she is doing. This means not only the small things like knowing and remembering things that are important to her, but going above and beyond expectations with surprises. Surprises need not be material things, such as trinkets, flowers or other goodies, although they will always be welcome. A reliable way to surprise her is to break with the usual routine. Get off work early and surprise her with the fact that you've cooked dinner and set a romantic mood for her to walk into. This will always get a good reaction, unless you're such a rotten chef that you've burned the crown roast. No matter, you've made the effort and started an evening that will segue nicely when you then take her out to dinner at a restaurant. Taking these steps shows that you do not take a woman for granted, and that's she's appreciated. And by giving, you get to keep the flow of circulation that is essential to the Circle of Giving and Receiving. Breaking with routine is good to practice on a regular basis, but don't overdo it. The value of being consistent with your words and deeds should never be underestimated. Be consistent but don't get into a rut with your routine.

What also will aid you in maintaining a balance is to purge your consciousness of previous notions of women in general. You're probably like many men and see a new woman you may potentially date as a replication of some cover girl from the latest flashy magazine or website trying to fire up your testosterone. Not only that, she must be sharp minded. It's probably not occurred to you that if this is the standard you hold women to, she's got a better mind than you do. The bottom line is if she's cute, sexy, and reasonably bright and thinks you've got something going on that works for her, you're miles ahead of the unrealistic dreamers that are going home from the clubs inebriated to cuddle and drool onto their pillows--alone.

Forget Everything and Start Learning

Unrealistic expectations are a big limitation on your thinking. You've just met a new woman, and there's a physical chemistry, a mutual attraction. This is always a good start, but men usually drop the ball from here. This woman has already gotten quite far being who she is, and your responsibility is to go find out exactly what that is. Likely she'll be a whole lot more interesting and appealing than the limited ideal you had to begin with. Don't ever underestimate the importance of a bright, cute woman who thinks you're a big deal. Think Less! Open your mind and your heart might just follow it, if you're lucky.

By now you should have enough of an understanding of what women respond to positively and negatively to traverse further down the Good Bad Boy path. Now is a very good opportunity to discuss something that every woman finds very desirable – *confidence*.

Before defining what confidence means, it's smart to know exactly what it isn't. It isn't bragging, boastfulness, conceit, self-importance, vanity, snobbery or arrogance. Fall into any of these behavior characteristics and women will likely crinkle up their noses at the foul aroma your personality is emitting, turn on their heels and walk away. If you don't know what the difference between confidence and these other less than wholesome attributes are, you need to learn this distinction right now.

If you need to boast about your job, possessions, boats, houses, bank account or other items of money, property or prestige, you're only kidding yourself if you think this is the essence of confidence. You are deluded if you think all this stuff makes you more attractive to women with substance. Not only will they be unimpressed, they will view you as someone who is pathetic. One great example of this was the story of a man who was vertically challenged trying to impress a woman I've known for many years, trying to get her to go out on a date with him:

One of his opening lines was, "You know, I'm someone who has a lot of money."

She feigned being impressed for a moment, and then said, "Really? Wow. So how tall are you when you stand on your wallet?"

He slinked away completely emasculated.

Confidence, as opposed to the above character defects, involves self-assurance. It defines a feeling of emotional security derived from a faith in oneself. Confidence is an instinctive certainty in your powers, capabilities and competence. Having confidence means you don't have to tell anyone how confident you are, it shows in your actions. It has nothing to do with what you do in the outside world, but everything to do with who you are – on the inside.

However, no male was born with confidence when it comes to females. Some are lucky and gain it earlier than others, and others hide behind their possessions and accomplishments and pretend confidence. Some never really gain it at all, and still manage to stumble into a relationship with a woman. Women find confidence in a man attractive, and they find a man that has confidence when it comes to women *really* attractive. Since males are void of this confidence to begin with, how are they possibly expected to become skillful with women? Confidence comes with doing things repeatedly and then finally reaching a point knowing you can accomplish what you've set out to do. You have to practice, practice, practice – and then practice some more. Good Bad Boys are always practicing, and as artists and students of women, are always honing their craft.

'Fine', you say, 'but what am I supposed to practice?' Since you now have a very basic understanding of the behaviors that women find attractive and the traits they abhor, it's time to venture out into the real world of pursuing women the Good Bad Boy Way. With patience, you will do a significantly better job of gaining the attention of women than you have been doing before. You are now going to boost your confidence in a way that you've never experienced before.

You are now going to learn how to properly seduce a woman.

Chapter 3

Seducing Women the Good Bad Boy Way

In terms of becoming a Good Bad Boy, there is nothing more important than becoming a skilled seducer. For better or worse, it is the man's responsibility in our society to do the pursuing, and the women have the role of being pursued. Like everything else, both sides of this dating equation have their good and bad points. I've heard many men whine about how they have to do all the work in getting a date with a woman, and like it or not, that's just the way it goes. You can complain all you want and fight it, and you'll spend a lot of time by yourself. You're more likely to hit the lottery than have a beautiful woman of substance come out of the blue and chase you down for a rendezvous. Look at it from the female side, they have to spend a lot of time avoiding low flying objects (men that pursue them that they want no part of) and I've heard many of them wish they could take the upper hand and just go after the guys they want to without all the nonsense. Some very confident women do this, but they are far and few between; this mindset is very much against the societal upbringing for most women.

So, like it or not, a Good Bad Boy plays the cards he is dealt, and in this instance, being the pursuer, he recognizes the fun and fabulous opportunity that is handed to him. By practicing Good Bad Boy techniques, there will now be access to a level of self-control in all interactions with women, so the frustrations many men have in terms of 'trying to read' women will be somewhat neutralized. By being much more proactive, men now have a fun opportunity to star in their own 'life movie.' This is a key point, for it will alter the ineffective dynamic that you've been operating under when engaging women, you are now going to start discovering what it is you really want, and then actively going out at trying to attain it. Don't concern yourself with the results now, they will come in time.

We're concerned about evolving as a Good Bad Boy, and developing the habit of regularly acting from within yourself towards women, simply by just being you. This will reap immediate benefits; you will be a man acting on how he feels, being genuine, and communicating in a forthright manner. By being yourself, and your actions coming from the inside out, you will be far less reactive and not find yourself trying to fit into a mold of what another person desires just to make points. More importantly, you'll feel better about yourself, you will strengthen your resolve and self-assurance, and all of this will just add to your allure and attractiveness to the opposite sex. The first step in this all-important process is to establish the foundation of seduction, and that is learning how to master flirtation with women.

Subtlety, Eye Contact and The Welcome

Flirtation is an art, and probably the single most important skill you must acquire and become proficient at if you are to be a Good Bad Boy. Flirtation can be one of the most fun and rewarding activities a man can do, if he does it from a balanced perspective with no fixed agenda. As with many other items, if you approach flirtation with preconceived notions and lofty expectations, you will probably end up very frustrated and feel completely outside of your own power. Expert flirtation starts with the very simple, but key concept that's been repeated throughout this book – *Less Is More*.

In all interactions with women it is always fatal if you appear to be trying too hard or are way too eager to please or make a favorable impression. An important notion to always bear in mind is that if you *appear* unconcerned (do not confuse this with uninterested) at first that will pique the interest of a woman much faster than if you take a direct route. Women have been getting hit on all their lives, and have heard it all, usually from guys without a clue. By simply a taking a contrary route, you'll get much, much further along. The route you will take is flirtation, the Good Bad Boy way. Flirtation is a 'getting to know you' process, but it involves pacing, subtlety, patience and the ability to think on your feet.

When acting through 'less is more', flirtation at first involves the skill of showing interest, but not showing *too much* interest. Probably a better way to put this is to not show too much interest too quickly. A huge part of you being attractive to women in general is that you are in control of your actions and emotions, that you are decisive and that you are clear on what is you want and how you are going about go get it. The first step towards all of this in the realm of flirtation is the initial indication of attraction – eye contact.

Probably the single biggest difference between men who are successful in attracting women and those that aren't is the ability to make effective eye contact with women. If you are afraid of women or lack confidence around them, it's likely you have a lot of difficulty looking a cute woman directly in the eyes, at least in a manner that is friendly and effective. Bear in mind, this is the initial indicator, and overcoming this obstacle is very, very simple.

Good Bad Boy Tip #5

If you see an attractive woman, look her in the eyes, wait for her to return your gaze and when your eyes meet, make sure you give her a friendly, warm smile. Seems ridiculously easy, but it's shocking how many men can't do this task effectively – if at all. Do not stare, and do not give her some grim, weird look. What you want communicated from your initial eye contact is "I'm an interesting guy who's worth getting to know better." Just be natural and wait for the green light before you proceed.

However, far more often than not, your friendly eye gesture and smile will not be returned to the level you probably hope. Get used to the real life fact that you are not all things to all women out there, and most of them will not share your enthusiasm for a little get together to know each other better. Generally women will catch your eye, and then turn their stare away; sometimes they will even smile politely before they turn their attention elsewhere. This is completely normal and to be expected, *it is by no means an indication of your lack of skills or attractiveness*. You don't want to spend your time trying to get the attention of a woman that is not interested in you, regardless of how cute she is or how you think the two of you would get along great together – even though you've not even talked with her yet! This is just part of the process of getting you connected with a woman that is genuinely interested. What you want is to find those women that are attracted to you, and they will let you know in the most simple of ways.

When a woman returns your look and your smile it is a good sign, a welcome and friendly return to your flirtation. However, remember that this doesn't mean that you're home free and a sexy first date is moments away! She may just be a flirtatious girl who's already attached that likes this kind of attention, she'll smile back at you as she walks on her way and gets on with the rest of her life. She also may just be polite and friendly and enjoy the interplay. Just because a woman returns your smile and is friendly in return doesn't mean she's thinking on the same plane you are. To really determine a potential match, it is now essential to engage a potential date in some light conversation.

Being Cogent

You can have all the eye contact, smiling and flirtation you desire, but you have to open your mouth and have some meaningful words come out of it if you're to achieve any level of intimacy. Again, as stressed throughout this book, keep the conversation simple. A commentary on the weather, traffic, and goings on in the area, and so on is a good start, but being clever is always good. You can even try a cheesy line like "If I had a nickel for every time I saw someone as beautiful as you, I'd have five cents" – as long as you deliver it in a charming manner with a smile – not with an agenda attached. You'll have to think on your feet and try to be friendly, but if you think too much you'll probably sink yourself. Don't over think, don't assume anything, you will almost certainly kill any chance you have if you do. Save the 'get to know you' questions for the first date, if you're skilled enough to get there. Your only task here is to determine if there is a mutual indication of interest, and you should know one way or the other after a short verbal exchange. *Just be yourself!*

A good example of this is that I was recently hiking on a local mountain trail near where I live, and it was an unusually hot day for late in the winter in Southern California. I was heading up a particularly steep part of the hill and noticed an attractive woman up ahead who was going slowly due to the heat and steepness. As I caught up with her, she looked back at me, and I just said in a friendly voice "summer's here early, sure is a hot one out here today."

With that she laughed a bit, smiled and nodded her head. I established a commonality with the situation surrounding us, a great way to start a conversation. If I chose to it would have been simple to converse further and get to know more about her, but my schedule was very tight and I moved on up the trail. The point here is establishing a common bond will be a great first step to the rest of the encounter.

It will be obvious if there is further to go with woman within minutes. You will *feel* the difference. You will know inside you that a woman is genuinely returning your conversation and eye contact in a way that shows that she's interested in you as well, just as you will know that she's being polite and not interested in you beyond a passing verbal exchange. The signs will all be there if a woman is showing genuine interest, the return of eye contact, a smile, questions or conversation that show interest. Make sure you pay attention to what's going on in front of you and stay out of projecting in your head! When all of these signs are there, you can happily proceed further. If not, don't waste everyone's time and move on. No always means no and if you think otherwise and try to change that, you'll do lots more damage than good. If you have to think hard about whether a woman is interested in you, trying to 'read between the lines' and so on, be assured there's nothing there for you, or at best the effort involved will not justify what comes of it. Bid a polite adieu and continue with your day. Your goal is to go where you are wanted and your attentions are welcomed.

If you are fortunate enough and get the green light to explore further, as mentioned earlier you will have to engage in some light conversation. It is important to note that this is a very key juncture; this is where a woman will get a first real impression of you beyond your appearance and what you say and how you say it. It will determine whether your time together will last quite a while with great fun and fulfillment, or only another awkward and uncomfortable five minutes. There are thousands of very, very attractive people in all the major cities who suddenly become very unattractive once they open their mouths and set their tongues wagging. Make sure you don't become one of the uninspired masses. What you say specifically is of course dependent on what topics come up in conversation, so it is impossible to 'script' a perfect encounter. However, there are some guidelines that should be followed here that will maximize your chances for moving this initial flirtation to a full blown first date, which is your only goal at this point.

Let The Cooler Head Prevail

Probably the most important rule at this moment is, no matter how striking, sexy, how she appears physically, how deep her eyes are, how well she is dressed – do not think *at all* about having sex with this person. Males regularly falter here, as they switch over to letting their hormones do the thinking for them. Your judgment will become clouded, and your motives will be transparent. Of course, for some, this is a staggering task, but it is essential that you put forth the impression that you are interested in this person in ways other than sex. Do not underestimate this! Do what you have to do, think of her as a friend, someone's sister who would kill you if you touched her, anything that gets your one-track mind off of bedding her. Besides, you're trying to determine if this person is someone you want to get to know better, establish a connection to help stoke the fire, and your preconceived sexual ideas will only get in the way of all of this. Good Bad Boys are always seeking a woman who is *sexy*, and being sexy is completely independent of appearance. Don't be mistaken, a knockout hottie with a sexy attitude is incredible, but there are many people out there, men and women, that look amazing, but they are anything but sexy. Sexy is an attitude, and it is carried by the owner with confidence. Becoming a Good Bad Boy is all about having that sexy attitude. You want to match up with a woman who understands that and operates from the same state of mind. A big part of being sexy – and more importantly, unsexy--is what comes out of your mouth.

So you're now at the green light, you've gotten a smile and an inviting look. Go and say hi. You'll likely get a hello back, but likely little else, at least at first. Attractive women get hit on all the time, and now you'll have to differentiate yourself from those that fell down at this point. For better or worse, this is an area that gets better with practice, although those that can think quickly on their feet and speak well will have an advantage. As mentioned earlier, you can trot out a corny line, but if you're charming and sincere you can make it work. You almost have to step outside of yourself and orchestrate the situation, think about your actions, words, what you're to say, what you are hearing. There is a reason why this is the stumbling block for so many, and why Good Bad Boys begin to separate themselves from others at this point. The irony is, as important as this point is, acting and really believing that it is not that big deal at all will serve you well. Just relax; the world will keep spinning, regardless of the outcome here.

Be deliberate, do not rush, think a moment before you say anything, this will help your mystique. A woman has decided that you're attractive and she's hoping there's something interesting upstairs in your head that will want her to investigate further. Don't let her down!

Good Bad Boy Tip #6

There is not that 'one word' or 'clever phrase' that will hit a switch and make her yours, although there is plenty you can say that will leave you by yourself. Just be easy, build up slowly; do not rush. Depending where you are, you can ask about the situation or location. If you're at an event, you can ask what brings her to it, what her interest in it is. If at a party, ask about the hosts, and her connection to them. Be upbeat and friendly; don't be negative. Negativity will kill your chances instantly, and mark you as a downer type of person. Most importantly, don't over talk! Most men suffer from this serious problem. You are trying to build a connection, and yakking about all aspects of your life will always do lots of damage. Listen and remember, <u>less is more.</u>

A key aspect at this point is to indicate a genuine interest in the woman you're speaking with, so you should be doing more listening than speaking. Remember the lessons from the previous chapter! Ask questions, but don't be obvious. Asking what kind of work she does is lame and uninspired. You want to know who she is, not what she does. Work life will come up in conversation eventually, and if she brings the topic up, just let her know matter of factly what you do, and move onto other things, you want to show you are interested in things beyond work life. Show interest, but don't be arrogant, if something she says comes up and you're not familiar with the topic, don't act like you know all about it. Admit you're not familiar with the subject--but you want to know more. This will get her talking and you can show interest.

You want to be doing much more listening and it's a bit of a poker game, but by listening you're collecting important information that you will be noting for later. Sure you'll need to chime in here and there, but brevity is essential. Just make sure your responses are more than monosyllabic. She needs something to work with as well! This is the kind of thinking and actions that will get you further. It shows humility, and women will *always* take a humble guy over a know-it-all. This will all require practice, and if you can convince a wife or girlfriend of a close friend to help you role play, you will get this all down much more quickly. She'll appreciate the gift certificate you give her to her favorite store for her time – generosity is a good trait to develop along with everything else!

Obviousness Is Never Sexy

If nothing else, don't be obvious. What this means is don't telegraph that the only thing coursing through your head is sex, like most men do at this time, and most times, for that matter. On top of figuring out what to say, you must be mindful of how you present it. Be respectful, polite, show genuine interest. If you are authentic in your intent and manner it will show, as well as it will be clear when you are being insincere. Good Bad Boys are artists, and like all artists, practice is essential. No man was born with all the skills of seduction; they are learned, and then practiced. While many times practice can be a chore, I can assure you that engaging in flirtatious banter with a cute woman is anything but work. Just get out there, be yourself and give it a try. This isn't calculus; even the most romantically unskilled fellow will be able to carry a polite conversation with a little bit of work.

Now, assuming you've managed to negotiate these difficult waters to this point, you need to know when to get out. Ideally, you'll just spend a few minutes establishing a bond, and then excuse yourself and get lost, so you can see her on a legitimate date. Now, if you should happen to have the good fortune of sitting next to an attractive woman on a cross country flight, or some other place where you're not going anywhere for a while, you'll have to pace yourself, and have several small conversations over the course of the trip and go back and forth between chatting with her and whatever you may have to keep yourself occupied. Always bring interesting reading material with you on trips, it provides great conversation fodder, and a chance for you to cleverly 'broadcast' some interesting aspect of you without you having to bring it up.

Alright, so you've had a short conversation with an attractive woman and you're feeling some simpatico there. There's flirtation, lots of eye contact, lots of smiling, a few laughs – because you were of course clever and witty in your few precious sentences – and everything is going great. So, now it's time to leave! It is quite understandable that this is against every cell in your body that feels it has the green light to move forward into some serious fun and games. However, one of the most important aspects of the journey to becoming a Good Bad Boy is knowing how to build desire in a woman in any particular moment, and at this moment you have a huge opportunity to do so. Anticipation is one of the most powerful aphrodisiacs, yet it is poorly understood and in our current society that puts so much emphasis on instant gratification, it is even more poorly utilized. You've made a great impression on this woman you've just met; now let it simmer with her for a few days. You want her thinking about you, wondering a bit about you, as you will be wondering about her. Just simply say something along the lines of "This has been really lovely. I wish I had more time to speak with you further, but I have an appointment that I need to get to now. I would love to take you out very soon and spend some more time getting to know you better." If all is going as it should, she will acknowledge the same and say that she would like that as well. Ask her for her number and let her know you will give her a call tomorrow to discuss a mutual plan and date. If you tell her you will call tomorrow, *make damn sure you call tomorrow.* Your actions and your words must always line up together, but it's especially important in the first few days of any connection. Good Bad Boys always work this way, without exception. There is no reason to have words and deeds at odds with each other. You will just appear flakey, and women will avoid you consistently.

Once you have the number, thank her, take her hand gently and drape it over yours as if you were to kiss her hand. Don't kiss it, that's just too Victorian and weird these days, but take your other hand and gently put it over hers so that her hand is between both of yours and give it a gentle squeeze. Look her straight in the eyes, give her a huge smile and wish her a wonderful day. Then gently let her hand go, turn and walk away. And do not look back at her, no matter how much validation you think you need! You have made a huge step forward on the path of being a Good Bad Boy. You're learning how to be attractive to women, and how to win them over with your words and actions. Now that you've made it this far, you're ready to take the next very fun filled step.

Chapter 4

Becoming a Seduction Artist

You've managed to secure the attentions of a woman who would like to see you for a first date, which is an admirable accomplishment, but now your work really begins. You have several days to get yourself into Good Bad Boy condition to be ready to move yourself and this potential lover onto the next level, and it will involve some planning. Hopefully you've had some practice at setting up a first date, but we'll go over it just to make sure.

Firstly, you need to nail down a spot that will provide a proper setting for your first date – romantic, sexy, a seductive environment. You may already know just the place, if not, with practice, you'll have a list of these places in your head and not have to think twice about it. Make sure it's someplace that isn't too loud or bright or crowded, too many distractions that interfere with making a strong one on one connection are to be avoided. Hip, trendy places are usually too much of a 'scene', but places that were popular a year or more ago (provided they're still in business), and are not as hot as they were many times is a great pick. Additionally, places with a nice lounge as well as dining is a smart choice, and make dinner reservations for a half hour after you plan on showing up. You can start the evening in the lounge over cocktails and after chatting and flirting for a little while, you can transition right into a nice meal, if that's what you both want at that moment. The point here is to make sure you have all the bases covered, and be able to offer choices at any given point. When you call your new acquaintance for your first get together, you want to offer several choices for her to choose from, as well as being open to take her to her favorite place, if she has one she likes to go to. Women respond positively and are attracted to men who plan these things and make sure everything is already taken care of. Good Bad Boys try to plan ahead and cover as many contingences in advance as they can. Women are attracted to a guy who has thought it all out ahead of time and has everything covered, because you took the time and made the effort to make the evening special *for her*. Once you have agreed on a place, be sure to offer to pick her up and drive her there and back, one because it's the Good Bad Boy way, and secondly it will help to make fulfilling the evening's goal easier – which we'll get to later. Often a woman will want to meet you at the restaurant instead of picking her up, which is an understandable safety reason since you are still a stranger. If that's the case, meet her there and for goodness sakes, *be on time*.

Losing Your Ego

So, regardless of whether you're picking her up, or meeting her there, you'll now have an evening full of challenges, risks and potential rewards, and you'll have to get the ball rolling by starting conversation. Again, the goal here is to learn about her, so asking her how her day went is always a good start. Again, there is no fixed 'script' to get you through the evening; you will have to earn your Good Bad Boy stripes through patience and practice. However, there are some parameters you should follow, and at the very least, it will make the learning curve a little bit easier.

As stated earlier, one of the big goals is to feel more and think less, and during a first date evening you will be sorely tested to think as little as possible. If you're spending a lot of time during the evening thinking about something clever to say, you're paying too much attention to what's going on between your ears and not enough on the cute woman in front of you. Big Mistake! What you need to realize is that your main goal is to make yourself as attractive as possible in these early stages, and while good appearance always counts, with most women it's *who you are* that really attracts – or repels them.

Despite how clever you may think you are, the more you blab, the less likely you are to come off as being attractive. It's just simple numbers, you have a better chance of surviving walking through a field with one landmine as opposed to one hundred, and you should view your conversation as the same, you will have to try to have everything you say really count for something. For starters, always take notice of how she looks, and be complimentary. Women always love getting compliments on their appearance, it's something that's hard to overdo. Do not be a doofus and say something awful like "You look hot" while you gawk at her.

> ### *Good Bad Boy Tip #7*
>
> *Good Bad Boys know ahead of time to look for certain visual cues – jewelry, earrings, lipstick, accessories, and comment favorably on them. She took time and effort to pick out something to make a statement, reward her by noticing it, because guys are always missing the subtle visual efforts when it comes to women. Keep it simple, such as "what a lovely scarf" or "that's a beautiful necklace". She'll feel it's an authentic statement and you've made an impression that you're different. You can delve further; ask her where she bought it, or if there's a story behind it, which often there is. This will get the conversation dynamic flowing and ease the comfort level.*

A woman will be very pleasantly surprised by the level of attention you're now paying to her and she will be very appreciative – and your stock will be rising quickly in her mind.

Since you're off to a good start, make sure you keep on track by staying out of your head, and drop all the agendas you may have. Spend time genuinely getting to know this woman. An easy question in any major city, since there are so many transplants, is the 'are you from the area, or did you move here' query, and from that you can ask all manner of questions showing your interest, from 'what was it like here as a kid' to 'what was it like growing up in _____?' Hopefully you're starting to get the idea. After a short while you'll be less conscious of what you're trying to say and actually be in the flow of the conversation, which is the natural rhythm a Good Bad Boy will seek. Conversation should flow, with interest, and sometimes each of you unintentionally interrupting the other, not out of rudeness, but more in the excitement of the moment. Be polite, kind, genuine, smile often, flirt with your eyes, and engage on many levels. Most of all, have fun with all this, it's important, but not a matter of life or death. If after a while you realize you've been bantering back and forth and a lot of time has slipped by without you realizing it, you've now stepped into the Seduction Zone.

Zen Seduction

Part of being in this Zone is being able to process information, and communicate it to your date in a matter that enhances your attractiveness. If you are dining, express how tasty your dish is, and have a small forkful of your dish at the ready as you offer her a taste of it. This assumes you haven't ordered something way off the chart, like sweetbreads or other esoteric cuts of meat. Save the adventurous menu choices for a much later time and don't stray too far from the middle of the road, but don't be too typical either! Hopefully she'll bite, so to speak, so you can gently place the fork in front of her, and she'll either take it from your hand, or hopefully lean forward so you can gently put it to her lips, and she can take it from there. Maybe she'll respond in kind and offer you a bite of her dish as well. Happily accept her offer and find what she's having tasting delicious, regardless of what she has ordered! All these small little things add up over a course of an evening, so while on the one hand you're paying attention to everything she has to say, you also have to be mindful of those moments where you will rack up the attractiveness points. This is the realm of Mr. Nice Guy, with the Good Bad Boy at his ear. So, just flow with your inner Nice Guy, we'll send him off later when he's no longer required.

Again we must invoke Less is More. Keep the conversation light and simple, inquisitive, fun and friendly. This is you getting to know someone for the first time, not a grilling for a job interview. Being too intense, obtuse or just plain weird will torpedo your chances. Your goal is to be as attractive as possible, and now is not the time to volunteer the extent of your baseball card collection, and so forth. You will have to talk to some degree, but don't try to over impress, just stay within yourself. Don't use words that can only be found in a thesaurus (you DO know what a thesaurus is, correct?) unless your date clearly demonstrates an advanced grasp on the English language – and assuming you can keep up with her. You'll know quickly if you've blundered off the path, you'll be getting a distant, glassy look back at you – your date has disconnected and you'll have to struggle to get her back. Part of the challenge here is seeking the common and comfortable level between both of you and that entails not only what you say, but how you say it as well. Guys are always in such a hurry at this stage – at all stages, really – but you must pace yourself. Coming on like the Running of the Bulls at Pamplona will rarely, if ever, gain any favor. Be engaging, flirtatious, make lots of eye contact, smile, but don't overdo it. It sounds tricky, but with practice it will all flow naturally.

One tact to take is to inquire about her status. There is most definitely a right way and a wrong way to go about this. Don't ask if she's dating anyone else, what she's looking for, what online dating sites she's currently on or any other ridiculous questions that will end the evening early for you. A flirtatious way of going about it is to first thank her for coming out and being with you that evening, which shows gratitude. Next you can inquire as to why such a special, lovely, attractive, striking (pick one, don't use them all) woman as herself is available. After all, you rarely find that someone of her caliber is accessible (make sure you say this!) and you were curious about it. Let her take it from there, she'll likely say something along the lines of not finding the right guy yet, she's been far too busy to date seriously, and so on. While being flirtatious, it is a polite inquiry to her status, you actually do want to know if she's just broken up with someone, ending a long marriage, or is a serial dater. These factors will affect the course of actions later, or sooner as each case may be.

Now, it may seem like trying to fill a couple of hours hoping to enhance your attractiveness through your conversation is a huge task, but you will be surprised what happens when a topic of mutual interest comes up. It all may seem like a frustrating form of twenty questions, but keep in mind what the goals are here, and that should help reinstate your incentive. You will just have to endeavor to find the right conversational topics, and try to think more like the woman in front of you, as much as you can. Make sure you avoid polarizing topics such as religion or politics, unless she happens to volunteer information and you are on the same page with her. That is a green light to proceed on that subject. If she happens to be a staunch conservative and you're a liberal's liberal, or vice versa, politely keep your mouth shut and keep those cards close to your vest. Differences like these can be problematic, but not always fatal, so let things play out. Ask what she likes to do in her free time, and hopefully there is some common ground there.

<u>Watch What You Say</u>

As much as you may avoid it, you'll have to show some sides of yourself. One of my fun diversions is to find and restore vintage BMWs, and I'm fully aware that it's not an interest shared by 99.9% of women out there. However, I'm *passionate* about it, and it's something I do because it comes from deep within me, having been around cars all through my youth. A woman may not share the passion for the subject, but she will respond to how much I love it and how it's important to me – they will feel how genuine it is. Do not be afraid to mention something you like to do, and that you love. If you get a strange response to it, she's not someone you're going to want to invest a lot of time in anyway. A really important aspect of these early moments in any relationship, regardless of what the parameters will eventually be, is getting to know who you are dealing with here. Regardless of what fantasies are spinning around in your head at this time, you must pay attention to what is being said to you, and what actions you are seeing, both from within or as a response to what you are saying and doing.

Families are often a safe topic, and inquiries to any sisters, brothers, parents, where they are located, what they are up to is usually a good strategy. You can glean a good amount of information from someone depending on their relationship with the rest of their family, and you can be sure she will be thinking the same thing about you as well. Particularly important from her standpoint is how your relationships are with your mother and sisters. Rightly or wrongly, a woman will make suppositions based on what you tell her regarding your relationship with the female members of your family. So, if there are any difficulties between you and your mom or sisters, now would be the time to soft pedal it. Don't lie about it, that's never allowed, but there's no need to get into any grisly details. The last thing you want is to have family baggage become part of the mix this early in the game.

Let's discuss an important distinction for a moment. There is no doubt that being honest is paramount, all Good Bad Boys know this. However, there is a key difference between being honest and being *frank*. I once heard a great definition on this, that frankness is honesty without the kindness. Fellows in relationships and marriages negotiate these tricky waters often, usually when posed with the no-win query of "does this make me look fat", or "how does this look" when a significant other is trying on new clothes. You can't lie, that will be picked up, but you can be diplomatic. Being frank is to be avoided at all costs, there's meanness underneath it that you never want to be associated with. No-win questions usually involve getting your opinion on something that's of particular importance to her. Be advised that this is territory filled with booby traps, and it doesn't matter whether the motivation is intentional or not. Good non-committal responses to any of these landmines could be "that's interesting" "I'm not sure", "let me think about that one" or "I don't know, what do you think", and there is also great value in saying nothing and just smiling. This way your date knows that you generally won't bite on those questions, so she may not ask again. You do not have to rush in and rescue someone of their particular insecurity at that moment. In fact, as a rule, it's a good idea not to do it at all in the realm of dating.

Despite your focus on your date, bear in mind a singular goal in becoming a Good Bad Boy is being comfortable with who you are, and being comfortable in what you say and do. Yes, you have to be attentive to the words and actions coming your way on a first date, but more important is the idea of maintaining your stature, being truly authentic to who you are and fully being yourself. Women have an uncanny ability to interpret subtext, and if you're phony in your words and actions they pick it up fairly quickly. Bear in mind, attractive women have heard every song and dance line ever uttered under the sun before you showed up, so you have nothing to lose and everything to gain by being straight and honest. You also would be shocked by how many women find the flaws in men attractive –

it makes you more human. You are spending time feeling things out on a first date, and certainly we all want to have an attractive woman be attracted to us. However, that is no reason for you to go against who you are. Do not be afraid to communicate your opinion if it differs from your date, you have a right to feel how you feel. What does matter is how you express it. Be respectful as to where she's coming from, just as you want to be respected yourself. Don't be combative, it's just an opinion, so be matter of fact about it. Trying to gain favor from someone by constantly agreeing with them will backfire, sooner usually rather than later, and a sharp woman will be suspect if you don't have opinions of your own, it shows a lack of strength. Obsequiousness is distasteful, and more importantly, this lack of intestinal fortitude will be viewed as weak, and that's *always* unattractive. A woman may not agree with what you have to say, but assuming your opinion isn't disrespectful, she should honor it. Show her who you are, there is nothing to be afraid of. Sending out the message that you are comfortable with who you are is something that women will find much more attractive than you trying to impress them by being a 'yes man'. Every guy has done that before and failed. Show you're different and that you'll be fine whether she likes you or not.

<u>You Can Actually Say No</u>

While you've spent good time and effort on making yourself appear more attractive to this woman, it's very important to realize that while dating is a boulevard fraught with hazards, it is also a two way street. You deserve to have some of this effort come back to you as well. If during the evening you're finding that no matter what you say, or what topics you're covering, or all the efforts you're making are just not getting anywhere, respect what's going on in front of you. Much more often than not, people just do not connect, and if you get that feeling inside--and the truth is always inside you- that this date is just not panning out, just be polite and let the evening ride itself out. Nothing good will come from forcing the situation, if it's not there from the get go, it's highly unlikely it will show up down the road. Men have that instant trigger as to whether they want to sleep with a woman or not, and too often it guides our actions. Women often feel that desire as well, the difference is that they generally don't let it guide them. For whatever the reason, there is just not enough in common, you have differing opinions on pets, she couldn't possibly date an Aries, and so on, there is nothing you can do or say to make a situation that is not meant to happen work. There's even the radical concept that despite the beauty of the woman you're out on a date with, after speaking with her for a time, you're not attracted to her anymore. Trust your body (except the penis, of course!) it generally knows when to move forward and when to move on--listen to it. You will be very surprised at how positive you will feel for taking care of yourself by listening from within. The empowerment you will experience from honoring yourself by declining to extend an evening with a woman you're not connecting with, regardless of looks, will feel fresh and rewarding; you will not hesitate to do it again when called for. Good Bad Boys take care of the women in their lives by making sure they take care of themselves first. Just remember there is amazing empowerment that occurs when you say No – in a polite, gentlemanly way, of course.

Hopefully though, at this point there has been a lot of fun banter, and there is a mutual attraction and some electricity is flying about in the air. You've accomplished a lot in this evening, and you should realize it is not a small feat. However, all of your smart conversations, attentions to her words, flirtations, eye contact and smiling back will all go right down the drain if you cannot put the capper on the evening. Whether you met her at the restaurant, or you are now about to drive her home, you will pick out that proper moment to show her that the evening was fabulous, that you desire her and you want to move your interactions to the next step. You will kiss her goodnight, and be aware that a woman can tell *everything* sensually and sexually about a man from that first kiss. You will show her in your kiss goodnight everything she needs to know – and can't wait to find out about more.

Chapter 5

Kissing and Keeping Your Balance

It is a clear truth that a whole lot is riding on that first kiss, like it or not. This will never change, so it's very important that you become *really* skilled at kissing. You already know if you are, so if you have any doubts, or just aren't sure, then you should assume you need work here. This is just one of those skills that you will know when you have it down.

The first challenge is the moment. It will be completely on you to make it happen, don't even think about a woman making this first move, you are expected to do it and will be judged on it, so accept the challenge and excel at it. If you arrived at your meeting place separately walk her to her car, or to where the parking valet is, or if you picked her up, walk her to her door. As you approach her car, or are waiting for her car to arrive, or are standing at her front door, let her know just how much you enjoyed the evening and that you would like to see her again, soon. You've already performed this task when you first met her and asked her out on the first date, so this should not be a big challenge at this point. If there has been a nice connection between the two of you, she should concur that she enjoyed herself and would like to get together again as well. Then, say something that acknowledges the connection, something like 'great, I'm very happy we're both on the same page' or something along those lines, put your own personal flavor on it. Then gently reach out and put your arms around her waist, and slowly pull her close to you, and look her straight in the eyes as you approach to kiss her.

If for any reason at this key stage, she doesn't respond in kind, gently pushes back from your embrace, turns her head while you try to kiss her, quickly and politely pecks you on the cheek, or any other indication that she is not ready or willing to give or receive a significant good night kiss, just accept it and back off, and wish her a good night upon parting. Any of these indicators show a lack of physical interest on her part, and you do not want to go where you are not wanted. For whatever reason, she's not interested in engaging with you physically, and that is a sign to call it a day with her and move on. It was a nice evening, enjoy it for what it was, and realize that the number of women that you will truly connect with is significantly smaller than the number that will pass on being with you. Trying to overcome any hesitation or perceived lack of interest with this person is time and effort wasted.

Good Bad Boys know that they deserve and desire to be with a woman who is attracted to them from the start, and who do not play games in regard to expressing that. The realm of dating and connecting is hard enough; having someone being inconsistent in their perceived desire from the start is a significant red flag. Call it a night and look elsewhere.

The First Kiss

Lets assume however, that she is happy to show her interest physically, which is an exquisite stage. There is a lot at stake here, so a few suggestions might help. Be very natural; don't come at her like a great white shark with your jaws wide open about to chomp on some prey. At the other end, don't keep your mouth too tight either, no one likes the feeling that they're kissing a desk, or have to bore their way in like they're drilling for oil. You should just meet lips, be firm but not overbearing, feel and kiss with your lips a little bit and then slowly penetrate her mouth with your tongue and meet hers as well. Be firm and exploratory, not too soft or wishy-washy. You're the guy; you should be firm, strong and confident. Mind you, these are just suggestions and general parameters, there is no 'one perfect' way to kiss. Feel the interplay with your partner, and let it flow. Luckily, doing it well covers a range, so you get to put your own personal touch to it. One of my personal preferences is to find a wall, or some other fixed object (parking meters work great!) that I can *gently* push a woman against so I have her pinned, unable to escape as I kiss her, leaving her little choice but to receive it.

The first kiss is as important as anything in the Seduction Universe; it is a glimpse to everything physical beyond it. If you are a good kisser, you will save yourself a lot of time and effort. As you are in the throes of this first kiss, do not rush, do not think, just let everything flow. If done right, time stands still while you're kissing. You are feeling, interacting, responding to what the woman is doing physically. Mix it up and change pace, pressure, pull back and do small gentle kisses along the perimeter of her lips, suck gently, or firmly on those lips and then gently go back in deeply for more. This is truly an art form, so enjoy it, and explore. You will have to work to define your own kissing style, but I can assure you practicing this will be great fun. Kissing is so important, and so overlooked in the dating realm, every guy is in a rush to get to the pot of gold. Pace yourself, in the end the tortoise won the race from the hare and the same principles apply here. If you've really kissed a woman properly, after a few minutes you will gently break your kiss and she should be in slight daze, breathless. In an old cartoon, stars or bluebirds would be circling her head.

Good Bad Boy Tip #8

If you've kissed a woman in a skilled, firm but gentle, extended and searching way, and she is seemingly tipsy afterwards, you've achieved your goal. She will absolutely want more of this, and you. At this moment, look her in the eyes, smile at her genuinely, wish her good night and then head off. You want the taste and effect of that kiss to last as long as possible, and you hanging around will kill that. The lingering effects of your kiss will strike a much more powerful blow than anything you can say or do (other than more kissing) at that moment. Get lost and let the power of your kiss and anticipation of more of that take hold in her.

Of course, as stated earlier, dating and seduction is a two way street, so it's important for you to realize if the woman you are kissing is skilled as well. Don't assume all women are great at kissing, there is better and worse here as there is in all of life. Often a poor kisser will also be less skilled in many other physical areas as well. It doesn't mean you should bail out on this woman, but it does mean you may have to have some patience over time and be willing to teach or learn together if you are interested and willing to explore and grow physically and sexually together. Bear in mind, though, you need to be at least somewhat accomplished in this art form before you start showing others how it's done, so until you reach that point, stick with the skilled partners.

Knowing Your Responsibilities

Now, let's take a moment and discuss one distinct possibility. The stars happen to be aligned in just the right manner on this first date evening, everything is clicking and there is connection and there's a nice charge between the two of you. You've given your date the kissing she was hoping for, and has stirred up a strong level of desire in her. It is just possible she may want to push the evening into deeper territory, and either ask you over to her place or want you to take her home to yours, under the understanding that things may become more sexual right away. In some respects, this is totally hot and very exciting, and your thoughts would lead to this being a very memorable evening. However, as a Good Bad Boy, you must check within yourself, and be clear on a few points that go along with the concept of having sex with someone you've just met.

Firstly, while you've just had a nice evening, and have connected in a romantic, sexy way, you are still dealing with someone who is a stranger in many respects, and you want to think about how sexually involved you want to get with someone you do not know. Keep in mind, a Good Bad Boy is in touch with himself from within and acts accordingly, and this situation could cause a very strong reaction. This could be an instance that many times plays out better in fantasy than reality. Since there is little connection other than your first date to go on, you can run out of common ground quickly. Physical intimacy should never be regarded lightly, and for all the concerns about taking advantage of a woman, being a player, and so on, how a man feels in this situation is just as important. A Good Bad Boy will wait and get to know this woman better, and bide his time. The added knowledge gained over a few encounters makes for a much hotter and passionate connection, and there will be opportunities to stoke the fire of anticipation and you'll be glad you waited.

However, there are those instances when it is obvious that the connection is just about sex and that it isn't likely things will progress in other areas. There are times where a woman is just interested in you for the sex, she's attracted to you physically, and is uninterested in a deeper connection. There can be a thousand reasons for this, and you are not to delve into any of them! The shoe is on the other foot, you are being viewed in terms of being a sex object, just as women have been for thousands of years. If there is a mutual attraction, then by all means, play the role of sex object and be good at it. Don't get into any discussions about what you can expect or what she is looking for, she looking for you to get naked and take care of her strong sexual desires. In other words, don't do any thinking at all, just go with the gift you're being handed.

In these situations, simply be attentive to a woman's physical needs, do not talk very much, other than asking her if there's anything she needs or wants. You're being used (in a good way, of course), and every one of your pals wish they were in your place. Don't make more of it that what it is, make sure the woman you're with gets your total 'A game' sexually, and be responsive. Once you both are completely spent, you'll probably be kicked out the door, or she'll quietly leave, more often than not these encounters have the meteor-like quality of burning intensely for a short period of time and then flaming out. You may have a few more get togethers of this sort with this woman and you may end up being 'friends with benefits" or her 'boy/man toy'. While these situations have value and can be quite fun, do be aware that they have limitations, particularly from an emotional standpoint. Don't expect too much as far as long term, however you never know where things may lead. As long as you and her have realistic expectations, everything should be clean and no one will get hurt – although there's never any guarantees on that, no matter how much you try to head it off.

Anticipation Redux

Often what you don't do has more significance than any action you may take. This is a key concept in *building desire*, which is the point you are now at. You've just parted ways with a woman after kissing her into a state of longing, and leaving her right there and doing nothing else. This is a strong foundation to build on. She will be thinking about it, reliving it (as you should be, too) all the way home. Now the both of you will be looking forward to the next time you will meet, and the power of anticipation again comes in. This was mentioned in an earlier chapter, and it bears restating. Anticipation is a powerful tool at your disposal; you want a woman thinking about you, wondering more about you. This builds a mystique about you. Let your good efforts simmer until you call her the next day, letting her know how wonderful the previous evening was with her. She will be happy to hear from you and ready to make plans for your next rendezvous. On this important call, which should always happen the day after if possible, be polite; let her know how much you enjoyed spending time with her and that you really are looking forward to spending more time with her. Schedule a next date with her, preferably on the next available Friday or Saturday night. It is also important that you again have a few choices for her, in case she wants to get into details. Usually you'll call back in a day or two to nail down the specifics, and yes – build anticipation.

The key here is that you are now the driving force on how everything will proceed. It will be up to you to come up with ideas, places and things for the two of you to do for the time being. Good Bad Boys embrace these opportunities for a number of reasons. You now have the opportunity to show your style and taste, and find places to go that will be fun, yet sexy, memorable and romantic so you don't lose sight of your goal. Now, while going to a show or out to a club dancing are fine ideas and would be fun, if you really want to become a master at the art of seduction and separate yourself from the rest of the dating herd, one of the sexiest things you can offer is to cook dinner and invite her over to your place.

The Good Host

Now, you may be challenged even when it comes to boiling a pot of water, but a quick visit to any of the cooking websites on the internet will reveal a lot of simple recipes, or you can hit your favorite search engine and put in the keywords "cooking, bachelor, clueless" and it should take it from there. And, and I've heard it said from someone much smarter than I in this regard, that "if you can read, you can cook". Women are used to getting taken out to nice dinners, and that's great, but the effort put forth by cooking a dinner for her means much, much more. Anyone can pay a dinner tab, taking the time to cook something she will enjoy is only going to enhance your stature and mystique, and further the concept of you being a little more unique among the dating masses. Don't ever forget you are always looking for ways to differentiate yourself from the hordes of single guys out there, and this is one excellent way to do it.

Of course, you may have to 'de-bachelorize' your living quarters, and enlisting the help of a female friend, or significant other of one of your buddies is strongly recommended. You just may be too attached to your lighted Chicago Cubs Wrigley Field wall clock to know that it needs to be put away for this particular evening, as well as many other possessions you feel are precious, that will compromise your stature as a Good Bad Boy. Obviously a thorough scrubbing is in order if needed, and that means dusting as well. A trip to the local newsstand and flipping through a few design magazines should give you an idea of at least the direction your place should be heading. Don't go crazy spending hundreds of dollars giving your living quarters a makeover, but spending the time making it a place where a woman will be comfortable and enjoy spending time will be worth all the effort you put into it. Make sure your place is clean, well presented, a romantic little escape that she'll be happy to come to. Candles and low lighting always helps, and playing unobtrusive mood music like jazz or other instrumental music helps set a nice tone for the evening. A woman will appreciate that you have a nice place for her to go to, someplace that's far removed from your fraternity house or college dorm days. Women, when they first come to a guys place are always sizing it up to assess his taste. Again, rely on the help of others more knowledgeable that you and take a trip to the local Target or Ikea, and pick a few key pieces and accessories. The money you spend now will pay off in dividends for a long time to come.

As stated earlier, you're more than welcome to take her out to an expensive meal or club; however the amount of distractions and noise in those choices could make it difficult to communicate and ultimately work against your goals. There is also one huge advantage to cooking dinner for her at your place that hopefully has occurred to you already. By having her accept your hospitality, you'll have gotten her to your home, which means you've taken care of one of your biggest challenges for the evening before it even begins.

Chapter 6

The Power of Your (In)Actions

Now, please don't become all full of yourself because you have a sexy, attractive woman coming over your place for dinner, and you think the cat is in the bag. You have a lot of challenging, hard work ahead of you, and your choices will determine how relations between the two of you will progress--or not. Your job now is to create a totally seductive evening, and that means making favorable impressions on all her senses. Your place has to look good, smell good--do your laundry- the dinner you cook should be tasty as well. Don't pick anything exotic or gamey or raw seafood, keep it simple and within your skills; chicken and pasta dishes are always a good idea. In asking her over for dinner, you were sharp enough to ask if she has a favorite dish, and assuming it's not too difficult and soufflés are not involved, go ahead and make it. Unobtrusive music will help with the aural aspects of the evening, and lastly, but most importantly, you save the touching and feeling for later.

Plan everything ahead of time leading up to her arrival. Making a nice, but simple meal will help, as complicated dinners with lots of moving parts are difficult to coordinate, and the last thing you want is her showing up while you're trying to tame a culinary monster. However, you do want to show off a little, so save the last parts of cooking dinner for when she's there so she can see you at work in the kitchen. Women love seeing a guy doing the work in the kitchen, they often spend a lot of time there, so it's fun for her to do the watching and be waited on for a change. All you need to remember is her seeing you handling things in the kitchen will continue to add to your attraction factor. Hand her a cocktail or glass of wine as you finish your cooking chores and ask her how her day was, and engage in conversation.

Inner Clarity

Let's take a moment here and discuss an important topic that could have a significant impact on what direction the evening goes. You can be sure that since your date for the evening has agreed to dinner at your place or wherever the next date location is, she is interested in pursuing things further with you and often with women that can involve an emotional component. That isn't the case every single time, blanket statements always are dicey when discussing relations between the sexes, however, it's a good approach to assume that there is that interest on her part, at least for the moment. Now it is time for you to check in with yourself on this topic. Women are much better than men as far as being in touch with how they feel, generally they'll know if they want to sleep with a man within a few minutes (not that they would do it that quickly, silly, they connect on a deeper level) but this is an important time to consider where you are with this person in this regard. This isn't about making a decision on marriage or anything as far-reaching as that, but you should have a sense at this point if the woman coming over for dinner is someone you'd like to date on a regular basis or you feel this will be a more physical, 'friends with benefits' type of situation. Just spend some time with that thought, and get in touch with how you feel. Once you have a good sense, file the information away. You'll need to remember it later, maybe even later this evening.

This thought process is important because it will help to differentiate between being a Good Bad Boy and being a Loser. Women love a Good Bad Boy and they loathe a Loser. It is vital you know what the differences are, as they may not be that obvious. Some of the differences have been touched upon earlier, but as things progress between a man and a woman, the stakes get higher and higher, and it is important to be more diligent on this topic as things intensify. We'll get back to all this in just a short while.

So, at this point let the evening progress naturally, be comfortable and yourself, relax and let things flow. Where many men get tripped up is having a big fat agenda in their heads, and letting it run the show. Yes, we all know there *is* an agenda there, and she is aware of it as well as anyone else. The important concept is to put it aside and not let it interfere. Just relax, chat and act totally as if your intentions are as pure as the driven snow.

Obviousness is not sexy almost all of the time. Get to know this person, show genuine interest and deepen the initial connection you've both established and progress it to the next level. Expand on the subjects you spoke of the last time, and spend time getting a sense and feel of the woman you're entertaining. Take pleasure in the evening by staying in the moment, enjoying your dinner and being engaged in interesting conversation. There is no substitute for practice, so just get in there, and start listening, asking those questions, building on the earlier concepts we spoke of. Keep being flirtatious, smile and stay connected.

Although it may feel like years will pass before dinner ends, it will end soon enough, and then be a good host and collect all the dishes and such and throw them in the wash sink, dishwasher, garbage, wherever your dishes go, and get on to the next phase. This is where things will get to be more fun, and you get to emerge as a Good Bad Boy. It is now time for dessert!

<u>Temperature Rising</u>

Once you have the dinner plates out of the way, or if you've been out to dinner, make sure you get close to her as you ask the next question. Look her straight in the eyes, and in a playful, but leading manner, ask her what she wants for dessert. Don't be cheesy about it, just straightforward, and flirtatious. You've sent a volley her way; let's see what she does with it. Now, a Good Bad Girl (that's another book) will usually come back with the simple reply of 'You' or something along those lines or even better just kiss you first. If you get either of those responses, consider yourself very lucky and move to the next phase of the evening. However, as often is the case, you'll lead the way, and build the fire. She may actually want a real dessert, so have some chocolate concoction on hand, or order what she wants from the waiter as soon as possible. Let's assume that to not be the case and she'll probably defer to you as to what to have for dessert, and of course, your response will be an emphatic 'You', at which point you will kiss her purposefully, and do it for an extended period of time. Then, get the check and find a taxi or get your car as soon as possible and get home – you have chocolate cake waiting at your place. However, if you were smart enough to make dinner, you can now lead her over to your comfortable couch, where the lighting is low, the music is nice and you can move on to the next part of the evening.

 This is where many a man has floundered and fallen. Here is the tricky area of potentially having sex with a woman, and being the nice guy you've always been, you don't want to do anything too forward, creepy or weird. However, the conundrum is that a woman will expect you to lead her to the point of sex, but ultimately the decision to move forward will depend on her having a comfort level with you--*feeling safe with you*--which depends on several factors.

> ### *Good Bad Boy Tip #9*
>
> *What is so difficult for most men to grasp here is how to drive the situation forward, yet stay out of making the decision, or forcing the issue. The crucial idea to be aware of is that in reality, sex will happen <u>only when a woman is ready for it</u>, and not any sooner. This is how it always should be, and is the only way a Good Bad Boy will have it anyway, because he knows at that point everyone is going to get what they really want. This is a key point in the evening, and the perfect time to let go of any preconceived expectations.*

You have already had a flirty, sexy dinner with a very attractive woman, so you're ahead of the game. If you expect more, it will come across to her in some manner or word and sooner or later and she will resent the expectation of sex, as any woman would and should. A Good Bad Boy is generous and gives without any expectation of sexual recompense. He has no reason to, and takes all the pressure off a guy feeling he has to get something back on his investment of time and effort. The reason why is a Good Bad Boy already knows how to make that happen, he is skilled at how to have a woman reach the level of *her wanting to have sex with him*.

Once you reach this point, things will become easier and more natural and you – luckily – won't have to think as much. However, getting a woman to this point is no mean feat.

So, you are now comfortably sitting at the couch, you've expressed your dessert preference, and you are kissing her, in the pronounced, sexy manner that you're getting better at by the minute. There now will come a few more dimensions to deal with physically, so you're level of awareness of what you are doing – as well as how she is reacting to it, needs to rise accordingly. Your kissing technique now needs to expand, and your kissing should start to gently, slowly move from her mouth, down to her chin, and along to her neck. Most women will respond quite well to you kissing their neck (unless they're really sensitive or ticklish there) and this particular piece of a woman's body and how a man can utilize it to heighten her excitement level can fill a book all by itself. It is very sensitive, so start with a gentle touch with your mouth and tongue, slowly and deliberately, and experiment with different pressure, gentle kisses on her neck, a little pressure on the jugular with your lips. There is a treasure trove of sensations here, so have at it and explore. You will know from her reactions as to what is working and what is not.

    While you are kissing her, you will need to have your hands be more active. There will now be more moving parts to the seduction process, but as an art form, it's time to progress to the next plateau. Be subtle with your hands, but purposeful. A couple of very good places are having a hand on her ribcage, thumb in front, and having some firm pressure there. Just have a good solid hold of her there, don't squeeze too hard, or move around too much, it can be a ticklish area. Another great spot is on her thigh, not too high up though! Again, a firm but not overbearing grip- part of what you want to communicate is that you are physically strong, but have a developed sense of touch, and know how to touch a woman, in the right places and in the right way. Explore the small of her back this way; there are almost always hot switches there. Use the same approach in running your fingers through her hair while kissing her, and gently hold the back of her head while gently pressing your mouth on hers while kissing – it will enhance the feeling that she's has no choice but to kiss you, that you are overpowering her, forcing her. Remember, you want to enhance the *fantasy* of this feeling, if you actually tried to physically force her to kiss you your evening will end abruptly and badly. The distinction with a woman is that she goes to that fantasy place of her own volition, you are just helping her get there with your actions, that she feels *safe* to go there.

Do not paw at her, or be all over her body on a constant basis. The idea is to touch and feel – not grab. As always, *Less Is More*, just have a firm, but subtle touch in a few different places, be easy, natural, and not in any rush at all. Do not start rubbing away at obvious erogenous zones, you will kill the moment instantly, as well as being viewed as puerile for doing it, which will send your stock plummeting. Communicate physically that you know what you are doing, are confident, and that there is no rush or pressure. This is the key concept here, and what is amazing is that each woman is unique, so you get to approach each woman as a blank canvas. Every woman has her 'hot spots', and when you find them, you will move things forward nicely to your goal of her wanting you.

The talent lies in finding those areas. This is a true treasure hunt, but be mindful that different techniques work for different women. A Good Bad Boy loves nothing more than discovering the nuances that make a woman go into overdrive.

<u>Being Naughty and Nice</u>

The challenge now is in the physical realm, there are stimuli and reactions going on multi-dimensionally, and you'll have to be aware of several different things at the same time. You'll have to keep kissing her, and using your hands to stoke the flames of desire that are building. The key indicator on all of this is how she is reacting to what you are doing. When you touch a certain place, in a certain way, if it elicits a short gasp, or a soft moan, you need to file this information away and know that you've hit a hot spot. Remember that spot on her neck you kissed and how you kissed it – and expand on it. Linger there for a little bit, but move on and find others. Guys are terrible multi-taskers, so showing you can handle several things at once again enhances your stature. The wonderful, yet challenging aspect of exciting a woman is that what drives one woman crazy may not work on another. It's all part of a Good Bad Boy's knowledge base, start from the beginning every time and find what works with *this* woman.

Start with the areas already described as a foundation and build from there. It is important at this stage to really be cognizant of what she is doing, how she is reacting to your kisses and touch. Any rapid breathing, exclamations of excitement – many women will just come right out and say "Yes! More!" when you've found some special place – Expand on what you're doing well, and drop those actions that are not getting a response. After some time, which may seem ages, things will reach a plateau, and you'll feel it. Everything in nature is cyclical, and the two of you getting hot and bothered on the couch is no different. Either the ante has to be upped, or the music stops. You'll now be a little more adventurous with your play.

There is no magic timeframe for this, you can get more sexual in 10 minutes or you can be kissing away on the couch for hours, the key is how she is reacting determines that. A woman can get completely fired up and will either express her desire to go to the bedroom, demand that you go there, walk toward the bedroom leaving a trail of her clothes along the way as a not so subtle hint or say nothing and grab you by the collar and drag you off. Suffice to say, those instances, although they do happen, are in the minority, so once again it's on you to turn the heat up.

Since the territory you're now entering is a lot trickier, you'll likely get feedback more quickly, and that is both good and bad. You may, as you are kissing away and exploring with your hands, delicately drop one of your hands to her lower inside thigh, and very slowly, subtlety, but deliberately, push her leg apart from the other, and hold it there, keeping her legs slightly apart. Or, you may slowly move your hand from her ribcage after a while, and run your hand over one of her breasts, and gently grasp it your hand, a delicately firm grasp, sexy but intentional. There is no doubt that both of these actions have an overtly sexual undercurrent to them, and as before, her reactions will determine how you proceed. She may react in a manner that you've hit a physical boundary and going any further will do much more harm than good. If that's the case, you need to respect this boundary, back off, and gently whisper in her ear that you're sorry, but you couldn't help yourself with her so close – or something of that flavor. It will get you back on track, but do be clear that you'll have to pursue the sexual component more slowly, and it is a likely possibility tonight is not going to be the night for it. If she continues to be excited by your skilled touch and her breathing and utterances continue to indicate moving in a forward direction, by all means, keep doing what you're doing-- Don't stop and think! You may want to rush things and get to the main stage, but you will make much deeper inroads by being cool, controlled, and deliberate – not reactionary to your hormones. Just spend more time stoking the fire and try to keep cool. Time will take care of itself, whether its tonight or another night soon. Regardless, in a moment you may have a decision to make.

Things are now at the brink of becoming sexual – or not. The difficulty here is gauging the situation, the moment and the people involved and trying to get a sense on it, and unfortunately there are no hard and fast rules here, since each situation has a chemistry all its own. First and foremost, be clear on where you want to go from here. We discussed earlier in the chapter about having a feel as far as what direction you wanted to go with your date, whether you wanted to have her as someone you date casually, or someone you want to explore more deeply on a one on one basis. Regardless of which direction you prefer to go, there is a vitally important item to handle at this moment. If you are willing, ready and able to have sex with this (or any woman), you now have the responsibility to effectively communicate what a woman can expect from you emotionally.

<u>Timing and Taming Desire</u>

This is someone you enjoy being with, and want to continue seeing, and get to know more intimately – you shouldn't even be at this point if this is not the case. So, respect, honesty and caring are in order right now. You may want to take the next step and be sexual with this woman – assuming she's ready for that with you, but you still want to keep your options open. Many, many men have this huge fear that if they tell a woman that they want to be physically involved with her, but you're not ready for full blown commitment, or you don't want to have strings attached, that women will flip out, be hurt, and you'll be shown the door, and you will have been a Loser/Bad Guy. The only way someone gets hurt is if you *don't* honestly state your intentions. Again, Good Bad Boys work from the inside out, and are true to themselves. One of the biggest revelations I had with women was when I communicated for the first time that I wanted to have sex with someone I had just started seeing, yet I still wanted to keep things open. Not only was she fine with it, it is how *she* wanted to have things as well. She appreciated the honesty; it wasn't something she experienced before, and all the pressure was off and we could enjoy ourselves. The important aspect is how you go about it.

Assuming that you've encountered no red lights from her at this point and there is a lot of heavy breathing and clothes are starting to come undone, you can slowly stop, pull back, look her in the eyes as you let her know what you are bringing to the table. If you're going the 'no strings attached' route, just let her know how much she excites you and that you want to take her to your bedroom. She may not hesitate for a moment, or she may balk, wanting to feel a bit safer. Let her know that it's not the time and place for a big 'relationship talk', but you do want to connect with her on a physical and sexual level. You add that you are willing to let the situation go wherever it's supposed to go, which includes commitment. There are no rules or expectations, just let nature take its course. Don't get into a big talk fest or discussion, you will kill the excitement. Just reiterate that while you are happy to go to bed with her, she is still free to go and live her life anyway she wishes without having to run it by you. If you do say that, you must also insert a little self-deprecating humor, like saying 'not that you needed my permission' or something worded along those lines, and say it in a joking manner. It will help the previous statement seem much less arrogant, lighten things up, and at this point you've acted in a responsible manner and are free to go to the bedroom, assuming of course, she's on the same page with you. It is very important to remember that women like sex just as much as men, and often want to pursue it, but they like anyone else do not want to feel like they are being used or taken advantage of. If you give the impression that you're only interested in sex, not only are you unlikely to get any, any Good Bad Boy will tell you that you don't deserve it as well. Desire the *person*, the rest will follow in its own time.

If on the other hand you find at this early juncture you are willing to roll the dice and commit your attentions to this woman only, that you're not even interested in pursuing other women (it happens!), then you have another route to take. You are at the same stage as above, all hot and bothered and on the verge of heading off to the bedroom. Every sexual cell in your body will be screaming at you to get down to it, to honor your primal urges and get physical as soon as possible, but you must not listen to them. Once again, stop slowly, pull back, look her in the eyes and let her know how you would like to proceed. Let her know that you find her very, very attractive, that you want nothing more than to take her off to the bedroom and ravage her. Hopefully she'll be nodding in agreement. Then let her know that, as much as you want her physically, you want to get to know her better, to establish more of an emotional foundation with her before you have sex with her. Let her know that you want to wait for a little bit. She will likely be very surprised by this; you may be the first man in her experience that has ever suggested holding off on sex when the opportunity was there before him. Make sure you reiterate at this time that you really want her sexually, that she is very sexy, beautiful, that this is hard for you to do but it is the right action given how you feel. This way she won't feel rejected, or that it's about her appearance. Ask her if that's okay with her. She may be a bit bewildered; this would be new territory for a lot of women. She'll agree, hopefully, and you can kiss her and thank her.

It is important to realize how powerful this course of action is. Firstly, as a Good Bad Boy, you've honored how you feel within, and obviously you wouldn't take this course of action if you didn't feel strongly about it, and her. Secondly, you have taken a route that she has probably little, if any experience with. You have separated yourself from the rest of the single male pack – far, far away. You have put how you feel about her, how you want to be connected with her, in front of having sex with her. Men will rarely choose this path given the circumstances. You have established a standing with her in a way that few, if any, men have done before. You have demonstrated in the most powerful way that how you feel is more important than your carnal desires. You have shown that you feel she is worth waiting for. All of these will deepen her regard for you, and you will establish a deeper place with her – instantly. And most importantly, by holding off sexual activity in favor of getting to know her more, you have turned the Flames of Anticipation into an inferno. Of course you may have done such a great job getting her all hot and bothered that while she agrees with and acknowledges your feelings., she simply wants you now, no matter what. You can go either way now, sex or no. with a clear conscience. You will now move forward as only a Good Bad Boy would, and should.

Chapter 7

Becoming A Good Bad Boy

Now, if the two of you have decided to keep things more on the physical plane and are going straight off to bed, you can skip down a bit, since the next passage addresses the route involving holding off sex for the moment. Firstly, give yourself credit for taking an evolved route in honoring how you feel inside. Also, realize that by valuing feelings over sexual relations with your date, you have most likely made a very great and favorable impression with her. She likely will want to see you again as soon as possible, but there is no rush, all the sexual activities will take care of themselves. You are now in a very detached, but powerful place of knowing you've done everything the Good Bad Boy way, and that you can now enjoy the anticipation of the next encounter with her. Have fun, but do take it in and learn from your actions, as they are the actions of a man in touch with his feelings, not a boy reacting to what his hormones are screaming at him, and that will always be viewed in a very positive light by the kind of women you want to spend a lot of time with.

Lovemaking as an Art Form

So, we'll fast forward a bit, if you've held off, you now are down the road, have had another date or two (which you are much more skilled at by now) and you have reached the point again where there is a lot of heavy breathing, furious, passionate kissing and clothes starting to go the way of the four winds. As before, do not take anything for granted and do not assume that just because you held off before that the both of you will automatically tumble into bed. Again, Good Bad Boys are skilled at having a woman reach the point that they want to have them, so keep gently, but respectfully, pushing the envelope. Be more sexual in subtle degrees, unbutton her top, gently push her legs further apart and reach higher onto her thighs – just keep gently upping the ante. Again, no obvious touching, save that for when you're both naked, which should be very soon. The suggestion of it all right now is much more powerful than doing it, having her thinking about sex with you is the most powerful aphrodisiac there is. At some point you both will be ready to explode, and it will be time to head to the bedroom (or whatever room you choose) and take your interactions to a significantly higher level. When you're ready to cross that sexual threshold, just look at her, and say something fun and naughty in a Good Bad Boy way. Something along the lines of 'are you ready to show me what a naughty girl you are?' will suffice, and then take her by the hand and lead her off to the bedroom. Or, she just as easily may not wait for you and lead you off on her own, lucky fellow.

There is no point going into specific sexual techniques, you're not fourteen anymore and it is important to develop a sense and style that is unique to yourself, and comes from inside of you. Anything else will eventually seem totally fake or forced. We will go over some concepts that will help set the tone and manner, but it is solely your responsibility to fill in the vast spaces that exist afterward.

Being a Good Bad Boy goes in stages, and each level involves more challenges, but there are consistencies throughout. Firstly, be deliberate, slow, and even though you may feel inside that your body wants to go at a supersonic pace, being in control of yourself will reap you many rewards. Women are very attracted to men that can control themselves physically. You are quite clear on what you want, or at least have an inkling, but as with many concepts that have already been discussed, being counter-intuitive will once again be the course of action.

By being selfless, attentive and tuned in with your partner, you will not only show that you are giving and willing to please, but you will also get exactly what you want – even if you're not quite sure what that is yet!

We touched on the power of anticipation, and being on the brink of sexual activity, all that anticipation is now rushing to your head. However, from here on, everything becomes very interactive. As with everything up to this point, your actions are predicated on having a woman at the peak of desire, and wanting you physically. Once in the bedroom, make sure this concept stays intact, even when the clothes come off, especially when you're with someone for the first time. Savor it like the fine sensual experience it's supposed to be, take it all in on all sense levels.

> ### *Good Bad Boy Tip #10*
>
> *Spend extra time feeling, smelling, tasting – this is no time to rush. View it as a sexual meditation, with all the deliberateness that goes with that. This will always work, and generally if a woman has reached the point where she needs more, she will usually let you know, and often times in no uncertain terms. Try to slow it all down – you will act more thoughtfully throughout and the sensual experience will last that much longer. All good!*

One sense I didn't mention was hearing. As it was previously in the throes of making out with her, you will need to heighten your sense of hearing, and really listen and sense what's going on. Every action you take will have some reaction, whether it's mild or wild. Listening to how a woman reacts to your sexual touch is crucial in learning what will work in terms of delivering ecstasy. Your touch with your hands or mouth may be too firm or too soft, and the only way you'll know is by listening and feeling to how she reacts.

A Good Bad Boy knows and loves the fact that lovemaking is an art form. While on the one hand it may seem very daunting and mysterious, it also reaps huge rewards for those that spend the time really learning the subtle nuances involved. Being skilled in this art will win you much adoration among women, given you're not a jerk about it (more about that later). Since a lot of men really are not very good at this, it's one more opportunity to separate yourself from the single male masses, which we've already established as an ongoing goal. More importantly, you'll feel great about yourself, and positive self-image and confidence really foster a positive upward spiral, and we want that to continue without end. So, as with any art form, practice as much as you can, and in this instance just take the opportunity and really spend time with her. Let your body catch up with your racing mind, and get back in sync. While you are learning with your hearing and sense of touch, do not hesitate to open up the channels of communication. This is not the time for a conversation, but do let her know, briefly, that she is welcome to let you know anything that you can do that will turn her on. No one expects you to know everything, and inviting her to express what works for her lets her know that her pleasure is as important as yours, and you'll continue to impress on her that it's actually more important than yours – which it is, since it's the key to many, many things to come, so to speak. Her hearing that you want to please her in a way that she wants will only strengthen the bond between you, and she will have a caring, considerate and unselfish lover in her bed, which is what *every* woman wants.

Still Listening?

When inviting her to communicate her desires and sexual wants to you, do let her know that she can express anything she wants, that it is totally open and everything is up for consideration. This will reinforce the feeling that it's safe with you, that she can be herself and not be judged or have some strange reaction. You would be sadly shocked at how many women have not had their desires and needs adequately considered, and worse yet, how regularly they are sublimated to the male's needs. Do not participate in this imbalance between the sexes, any clueless male can, and does, proceed this way, and Good Bad Boys take the higher, evolved path. Once more you can differentiate yourself, find out what really gets her sexual attention, and be willing to go forward with it enthusiastically. Of course, since you offered open communication, do be prepared for what may come back to you. It would be unusual for things to suddenly turn wild or kinky, but in the realm of sex there are few limitations. She may have a long harbored fantasy that no one has ever indulged her in, so be the first to do so. This assumes, of course, that you do not do anything to harm yourself, or your stature, do not suddenly turn off the Good Bad Boy path. If something strikes you as too scary or outré, just offer to revisit it at a later date after you know each other more, which values her desire but allows for things to progress more safely. However, do be willing to stretch yourself. If she wants to engage you sexually while you recite the poems of Shelly because it's a huge turn on for her, by all means go for it.

Enriching your experiences only adds to your body of knowledge, and in the art of lovemaking, you always want to be a student. Listening leads to learning and putting what you learn into practice builds a strong foundation of confidence. While every woman is different, listening, learning and receiving from them the lessons they offer will enhance your standing with womanhood as a whole. Besides, this is all supposed to be fun, so take the load off yourself. Find out what it is that will drive your woman wild, and then do it.

As this should be one of the more fun learning experiences in your life, share it with her, and make sure to reinforce that she can communicate her needs and wishes with you at any time. You are just learning about her physically, and it's very unrealistic for you to know every little nuance and place that will send her to the next level of heightened sexual pleasure. She will tell you if you offer the invitation, so make sure you allow for that communication path. It will enhance your connection, and you'll be a much better lover as well, which is one of the most important goals throughout this process.

The Power of Physical Knowledge

A woman's body and how it reacts to sexual stimulus, is one of the most fascinating subjects for a Good Bad Boy, and compared to a man's body, it is a veritable wonderland of magic places. Discovering them and learning to enhance the physical experience will be a very satisfying journey for the both of you. Men, in most respects are very linear and very happy to go from point A to point B in a straight line. This is not how you want to interact sexually with a woman. Women are much more circular, and the physical journey involved is very, very important. Bear in mind, once a man climaxes, the party usually becomes a whole lot less interesting for everybody. A Good Bad Boy will hold off his pleasure to make sure the woman he is with is fully satisfied. Taking the time to learn and then using that knowledge to bring a woman to sexual satisfaction, is the responsibility of all Good Bad Boys. One shouldn't get into the mindset that if a woman doesn't orgasm, then you've failed. Sometimes it's just not in the cards, but one should always be willing, ready, and able to do what is necessary to fulfill and satisfy the woman you are with every time you are with her. Again, let everything flow naturally, do not rush, the last thing a woman wants to do when she's with a skilled lover is rush to orgasm. She's having a fabulous journey and she wants the trip to last as long as possible, and in order for that to happen, you will have to be very good at physical self-control.

This is probably the biggest challenge and point of contention as far as sexual activity between men and women. Most complaints that women have with men physically is that they do not last long enough for them to be sexually satisfied, and they almost never can express their disappointment with this, since it's such a delicate topic. This is unacceptable for a Good Bad Boy. The Fragile Male Ego and all that nonsense needs to take a hike, and men need to learn how to properly use what nature has gifted them with. Once again, here is an opportunity to differentiate yourself, and it is the most important way you can do it. Learn self control. There are probably a thousand different ways of doing it, but whatever works for you, start doing it, and keep practicing. Some men are lucky enough to have this ability naturally, but they are few and far between – just ask any woman. In fact, probably the most important skill a male can have in the adult video industry is the ability to have self control, and to be able to orgasm for the 'money shot' on cue. With practice, it can be done. The practitioners of Tantric sex are skilled at this, and they spend years learning how to sublimate the physical urges that dominate a man's body while in the middle of sexual activity. You need not become a Tantric Master to be skilled at self control, but some of the characteristics we've already discussed should be employed here.

Good Bad Boy Tip #11

Firstly, breathe, and breathe deeply. It is a relaxing technique, and being relaxed and unrushed, physically, mentally – in every manner – is the way to go. Next, take a lesson from women and focus on the journey, not the destination. Men are overly fixated on getting to the point of climax, and they miss the opportunity of rounding out and expanding their sexual experience. Keep relaxing, and focus on where you are in the exact moment, and not where you want to be.

Again, let things flow naturally, and take a lot of time doing this. Also, you must learn how to be comfortable with the sensations in your body and not letting them overtake you. One of the most pleasurable feelings I've experienced is being on the brink of orgasm – and staying there for as long as possible. It's hugely satisfying, almost as much as a climax and it lasts a whole lot longer. I just relax, close my eyes and try to 'get inside' my body, just feeling everything, and thinking as little as possible, and maintaining a steady rhythm throughout.

The key here is for you to find that 'space' that you can stay in physically, while all this sexually charged stuff is happening. Once you arrive there, you will know it, and relax there for a long time and enjoy all that is happening, because this is the physical place where all skilled lovers spend as much time as they can. However you do it, and there are as many ways to do it as there are men, get proficient at this as soon as possible. Women value men who have sexual self control very highly and those boys that don't are relegated to the slag heap of non-performers. Become skilled at this and the woman or women in your life will be very happy with you. A general Good Bad Boy rule is make sure you bring your woman to climax first, and then it's your turn – ladies first, as any gentleman would tell you. If she's multi-orgasmic, lucky you and you'll just have to wait until she's had her fill of you – hardly a sacrifice. You've worked very hard to get to this place that feels really good, in many respects. Reward yourself by making it last as long as possible. The rewards will be great.

This is just a smaller, self –knowing aspect of the bigger topic of physical knowledge. You have already spent time finding out some of the physical places that turn a woman on, and getting to know your body more intimately and getting comfortable with it. Now that a foundation has been established, just simply explore and experiment from there. Try different things as an easy, natural extension of where you are at. Sex is a big playground; find what works, and what doesn't, between the two of you. This is one fact finding expedition you will love to be on.

<u>Going Mental</u>

Once you feel you are on solid ground from a physical standpoint, you have an opportunity to add a very exciting dimension to your interactions. This is an area that can be hugely rewarding to experiment with by bridging the gap between the physical and the mental. It's often been said that the most important sex organ is the mind, so time to explore it. While you are doing your happy duty physically and she is writhing around from your skilled actions, there is a festival of fantasies playing around in her head. It's not that she's disengaged from you; women just add this element for themselves, particularly when their heads are thrown back and eyes closed. They are on their journey, in a hot space that their fantasy minds create. Men usually are engaged on the sexual activity going on right in front of them, women rely more on what's in their mind and body. Sure, they go back and forth and check in on what's going on in that moment between you and her, but it is usually to add fuel to the fire that's already going on between their ears. Now is a great time for you to not only join that fun party going on up there, but to make it even more of a turn on for her.

Adding to the mental aspect of sex is most easily done verbally, and being an added dimension, the stakes get higher, things are more challenging, but the rewards are greater as well. So, as lovemaking is an art form, here is a chance to expand your creativity. As you become more comfortable with your physical lovemaking abilities, start experimenting with different dimensions, and the verbal aspect is the best place to start. By engaging her in 'conversation' it will just add to the heat of things. Avoid having this word play be anything deep or something she'll have to think about replying to you don't want her mind off of all the other fun things that are going on. Remember, Less is More. The specifics of what the two of you say can be far ranging, but you can always start with statements such as "You're a naughty little girl, aren't you?" and other innocuous, yet spicy comments that will usually elicit a simple, breathy "Yes!" from her. You want your words to add to the mix, not take over or get in the way of anything that's going on. Try not to be cheesy about it, although if you say something that just has her bust out in laughter, which could easily happen, just laugh along for a moment, then get back to the physical matter at hand. A little laughter together through this is a good way to connect, sex should be fun, and so many men take it so seriously and put huge amounts of pressure on themselves, and their partners. Do your part to keep the fun in it all.

How To Be a Good Bad Boy

The concept to understand here is the delicate but crucial balance of being a naughty seducer, a Bad Boy, yet providing an environment where a woman will feel safe with you, emotionally and physically. This balance is Naughty AND Nice. Your Inner Nice Guy provides the safe environment--you already know that drill-- and the Good Bad Boy comes in and starts pushing buttons and turning dials with his lover and sees what results come from it. Be playful with your words, but always try to enhance the moment, let her know you're a Good Bad Boy in word and deed. Getting her to confirm your observations on what a bad girl she is almost always is a good place to start.

Sometimes a woman wants no part of hearing what you have to say, it's more a distraction than enhancement. As with experimenting physically, there will be things that cause fireworks and things you say that will not work at all. If this is the case, she's not someone who responds to verbal play, so you'll just have to explore further and find all those things that do get her really hot and bothered. There are worse crosses to bear, believe me.

The biggest point of all of this is that there is a strong chemistry developing between the two of you, and your responsibility is to be observant, and act on what you discover. As stated earlier, Good Bad Boys are always students, there is always more to learn, and keeping your mind open, a willingness to experiment and try different things will move you down the path of Good Bad Boy evolvement very quickly. Just keep practicing, and learning and discovering. This will be a very rewarding endeavor for you and the women in your life. While it all may seem a bit much and you may feel clumsy at first, each time you will gain more and more knowledge, and your confidence and self esteem will grow. You will feel great about yourself and learn to love flirting and knowing women more intimately. Try everything, and go with the flow and accept with grace what works and what doesn't. Life will become very, very good.

Chapter 8

Evolving as a Good Bad Boy

After spending some time practicing and interacting with women in the Good Bad Boy way, your level of physical and sexual confidence will increase significantly after a short period of time. Women will still have many mysteries about them, but at least you'll be much more aware and able to connect with them physically and sexually in a very confident manner. The knowledge you have learned and developed through practice and heightened awareness is precious and powerful. What you have to also bear in mind is that there are a lot of responsibilities that come with this knowledge, and how you behave from here will say a lot about you, and whether you truly evolve into a Good Bad Boy.

Being a Good Bad Boy is much more than being an attentive, skilled and confident lover. Be assured, those attributes are necessary and very valuable, but who you are and your attitude around all of it is every bit as important. While you may have caught the attentions of women in a special way, that doesn't automatically make you Mr. Desirable to every woman that's out there. Guys in general are attracted to a wide range of women, whereas women are much more selective.

Go Where the Lust Is

Everyone has their tastes and preferences, and while you've come a long way, there is simply nothing you can do if a woman doesn't click with you on that instant, primal level. Its there or its not, and if its not you need to respect that and leave it be. However, it is important that you give yourself as much opportunity as possible to make that connection happen.

It is important to know who your potential audience is and make sure you're as attractive and accessible to them as possible. While you don't have to take out a second mortgage for new clothes and other appearance enhancements, spending time on how you will look to someone you're interested in is time well spent. As we mentioned earlier, getting the suggestions of your women friends is always a good idea. It's easy, since women generally think men can barely dress themselves, so they are happy to give their suggestions. Be smart and follow them, they know what they are talking about and you are getting the exact information you need. Get feedback on your most and least attractive physical assets, and take them to heart as we are all not very objective with ourselves. You'll have to enhance the positive and downplay the negatives. It will feel odd and uncomfortable at first, but remember, if you want to be a Good Bad Boy, you will have to sacrifice some old ideas about how you should appear in the world to make yourself more attractive to a bigger slice of the female population. The first impression you make on someone is your appearance, and while you could overcome a lack in appearance eventually with charm and panache, it's far easier to look well turned out, and build your charming style on top of that. I've lost count of how many times I've run into a very cute woman in my free time and began to engage her in conversation, but since I left the house unshaved or poorly dressed, I had to start from a weaker vantage point. I had to work extra hard to overcome those negatives that I didn't take a few minutes to address at home. Ultimately, I overcame them, but why make a tough challenge even harder? Bottom line is you never know when you are going to run into a very special woman, so you should *always* be prepared. It adds to you as opposed to having to counter something negative, so you're working smart for yourself.

As briefly mentioned before, despite your appearance efforts and making best use of what you've got, you will not make every woman perspire with anticipation when you walk into a room. In fact, you will not catch the eye of *most* women when you walk into a room, unless you really possess Hollywood leading man looks, and even then it's touch and go. The good news is you don't have the time or capacity to handle all of that attention, despite what you may think, and catching the eye of even a small percentage of the women you come across still translates into a large number. The reality is that trying to date more than two or three women at a time, as much fun as it may seem in your head, would start to work against the quality of your life, as you would find little time to yourself and being much more reactionary to your social life, as opposed to actively defining it. You'll be less happy with more women and happier with less, even though that seems counterintuitive to almost every male out there. Once again – Less is More. Get one at a time down first and then you can concern yourself with adding more if that's your interest.

Since you don't have to worry about appealing to the masses of women out there, your task now is to find those few that you will really connect with. The hardest part of this is the patience involved because a woman who wants to get closer to you will let you know it, but in a subtle manner. Your task is to make sure you're alert enough to pick the signal up when it is sent your way and be ready for it, regardless of how long it takes. This simply means is you go about your normal routine, and at all times be prepared to hone your Good Bad Boy skills. Instead of being like most men, trying to impress yourself onto a woman that really isn't interested, you'll patiently wait for one that is interested in you to show you a sign. Mind you, you have to have your radar on all the time. You have to be proactive, and practice all the things we mentioned during the early dating scenarios--making eye contact, smiling, being ready and able to drop a clever line to get things rolling – but after that, you step back and wait for the green light, whether it shows up or not. This is important for a Good Bad Boy, since you only want to go where the lust is, and not where you're uninvited. There is no timetable for any of this, you can go weeks without any positive responses or have two women show they're interested within an hour. Consistency is the key, and of course letting go of any expectation as to when and how it's all supposed to happen.

The High Road of Quiet Confidence

How you carry yourself through each of your days is now important. You have more confidence now that you've been fortunate enough to gain some understanding on what women are looking for when initially encountering a man. Let this quiet confidence permeate through all your words and deeds, particularly with the opposite sex – it will add to your attraction. If you are to truly evolve as a Good Bad Boy, you are to take your new found knowledge and modestly hold it in reserve until it's called for. The worst thing you could do at this point is misuse your new skills and become a jerk. Alas, this is a very easy thing to do.

There is a fine line that runs between confidence, conceit and arrogance. Be charming and playful in your interactions and hint at what you may have in store. Acting like you're a complete stud and everyone should honor you for it is completely gross. You'll be just like one of those Neanderthal single guys that used to roam the discos in the 1970's with 10 pounds of gold chains blaring through shirts open to their fat stomachs. Women have mastered the art of being mysterious, so you'll do well to be modest, play things close to the vest and let a woman discover all those fun things about you as well. This is balanced and both parties will enjoy the hunt. Just because you think you know how to bed a woman doesn't mean you now get to do it any faster, you still have to take the time involved to properly interest and seduce a woman – that will never change. If you go back to the old thinking of just trying to get a woman into bed as quickly as possible, even with your new knowledge, not only have you failed all the lessons we've discussed, you've actually regressed, since you are now *supposed to know better*. You're on a new path now, there is no turning back – moving forward is where the rewards are. Be modest and humble, and show all the caring and concern we discussed in the earlier chapters, these are attributes that are now permanent.

Additionally, it is very important to spend some time examining how you are to behave moving forward with someone you are now intimately involved with. This is not alluding to a relationship discussion, which will be touched on more in the final chapter. You've already been clear with her on what she can expect from you emotionally, and until that changes on either side, you keep the lines of communication open and behave in a manner that is consistent on what you've told her to expect from you. Anything short of this is not Good Bad Boy behavior, it is furtive and disrespectful. A lack of forthrightness and being honest and timely in your emotional communications will hurt those you interact with, but most importantly, the person you will damage the most will be yourself. You've put a lot of time and effort into being a man that women want to be with, so you now must *always* take the high road – there are no exceptions.

How To Be a Good Bad Boy

The point that most men miss, and that Good Bad Boys already know, is that if you are caring, honest, communicative and respectful to a woman you are involved with, regardless whether you've been together ten days or ten years, you will have available to you everything you desire physically, and then some. Mr. Nice Guy has to have his place and here is where he is best utilized. Once a woman feels that she can depend on you emotionally, it will be much easier for you to lead where you want to go physically. Spending the time establishing this base of care and trust is vitally important, regardless of what the relationship dynamics are. This foundation must be in place to be able to fully explore your Good Bad Boy potential and possibilities. There is no secret to all this, just be a decent, honest, communicative, 'stand-up' guy – for some reason these men don't seem to come along that often, so once again you've differentiated yourself from the herd. Most men are afraid to directly and honestly communicate how they feel to a woman, for fear that what they may say will upset them and ruin everything. I can assure you that not saying what you feel will do far more damage in time. Be a Good Bad Boy and always say how you feel – in honest, caring terms, of course!

With a bit of time you will know your partner better and have an idea of what works sexually and where to explore and where not to. Obviously communication is the key to all this or it will take much longer than necessary to uncover important facts. Some of this is trial and error, getting the balance between being a nice guy and being a naughty seducer that women want to succumb to takes practice and is different with every woman. Considering the rewards, this practice is time well spent, and it's not exactly an onerous task. The best attribute you can exercise to further your goal is to be patient. We've discussed this earlier, but it can't be overstressed.

Being True to You

In the big picture a Good Bad Boy is trying to act on his feelings and go from the 'inside out' as opposed to reacting to whatever stimuli is coming at him. As earlier stated, Nature always exists in balance, and you are to do the same. It will take a little time to properly juxtapose your inner Nice Guy with the Good Bad Boy, but it will come in time. The only way is to do it, and you will be very surprised at how open your partner will be if you've provided a safe and respectful environment for her. The biggest challenge men have had to face in the past 40 or so years is the contradiction of women wanting to be treated as equals in every aspect of the everyday world – which is appropriate and desired – and the fact that many women look to be guided by a strong male presence when it comes to physical intimacy. It has proven to be an impossible chasm for most men, and the only way to bridge it is to have the Nice Guy and the Good Bad Boy know their places and call on them when the time is right.

Despite the appearance that this is all very mysterious and difficult to intellectualize, at least from a male perspective, if you show a woman you are involved with that she is important, you will avoid many difficulties. These are basic rules that have been already discussed, but you may have already forgotten them! Be attentive, caring, nurturing, and make the woman you are with feel like she's number one with you, even if your mutual understanding of your relationship is casual and non-committal. Being present and reliable, and having your words be consistent with your actions, will enable you to avoid having the 'Player' label slapped on you. Good Bad Boys never want to be called that, even in a ribbing manner, the undertone of the Player definition implies that you are only interested in having sex with a woman and that all the other important aspects that round everything out to a fulfilling experience are of no importance. It is imperative that you avoid being viewed in these terms at all costs. If a woman feels you are really a Player, she will keep you at arms length, because Players are just simply Bad Boys, despite all the sugar and charm they may pour over on a woman they're trying to seduce. Players often times are selfish jerks that border on misogynists. Have your actions and how a woman views and feels about you be as far away from the Player label as possible. If you shortcut any of the topics we discussed up to this point, you run the risk of being viewed in these very unpleasant terms. Don't stray from the Good Bad Boy path.

<u>The Most Important Destination</u>

One of the most significant goals you will strive for as a Good Bad Boy is to secure a special place in the heart of women you are involved with, regardless of what the commitment level is. Men mistakenly have the notion that it's 'all or nothing' with women, that you're either emotionally aloof, just a 'friend with benefits' or completely committed and monogamous. Women cover much more of a spectrum emotionally and what they are looking for can cover a very wide range, so don't assume anything, just let it be revealed to you. What matters is that you act like a secure, confident man around a woman, particularly in regard to sexual matters. If you are forthright throughout, regardless of the level of involvement, you will always be held in a fond regard by a woman, and this is a worthy goal. Most of the time it is the very simple idea of being a decent fellow and by now this should be standard operating procedure to you. You're not (hopefully) a jerk to your guy friends – so give the women in your life the same benefit, and you'll gain much more than you expect. Developing a relationship with the woman that you've been intimately involved with into a close confidant and friend is a rare and special situation. You can have someone who knows you in a unique way, and be able to offer counsel and suggestions that come from a place that your other pals will never be able to approach. You will always be adored by this woman on some level, and adoration by a woman is a very worthy accomplishment that most men do not achieve, much less appreciate.

This is a special reward for being a Good Bad Boy, over time you may have several women that you can rely on for a special perspective on things, and their take on your life is something, like all input from your support network, to be valued and considered.

It is a unique friendship and one that has a special level of trust, as well as a level of connection that will always be there. Cultivating these long term friendships, with or without the sexual component to them, is well worth the effort. The only caveat is that over time people do get involved in more committed relationships and an old lover's new boyfriend may not appreciate your 'special' friendship, or you may have a new committed relationship and she may feel uncomfortable with a past flame as well.

Good Bad Boy Tip #12

Honoring the relationships you've committed to will always take priority. There may be the rare instance where your current girlfriend has no problem with this, or may even want to get to know your old flame. Don't count on it though, the far majority of the time 'exes' are less than welcome. Keeping the women you currently or previously have been involved with separated from each other is a very safe and healthy habit.

As a Good Bad Boy, you will have special knowledge and skills, it will almost seem like you are privy to the most obvious secret in the world that is right under every guy's nose. However, that does not give you license to flaunt it or act like you're better than every guy out there. We've mentioned that being full of yourself is a turn off, and that will never change. There is no room for complacency on the Good Bad Boy path. As soon as you think you've 'arrived', you need to take stock of your attitude. Humility is the only attitude to have, and when that is coupled with sexual confidence, you have a combination that is irresistible to many,

many women. Besides, it's much more fun to think that there are unlimited sensual delights out there waiting for you to discover, and you'll never find them all! Simply take on a very basic mindset that was touched on earlier in this book, and one that many spiritual teachers advocate. Be focused on the journey, and all the rewards that you'll uncover along the way. Good Bad Boys already know there is no 'destination' or 'finish line'; all the satisfaction and fulfillment comes from the process, from all that you experience and gather along the way. You never want to be so blasé that you really feel you've 'been there and done that' sexually. That would be a bore. There is *always* something new and exciting awaiting you, whether you've just started this process or have been in a committed relationship for years. It all comes from a humble attitude, and knowing the world out there is a whole lot bigger than you are. If you truly acquire this refreshing take on things, most days will feel like there is some great new surprise out there waiting, and it's the difference between living a full life and merely existing. You have the choice, so which one do you prefer?

The Power of Persuasion

As a Good Bad Boy you will also develop the ability to be a coercive influence. Once you take the time to make a woman feel special, safe and desired you can really explore. Assuming you're with a woman that has a pretty extensive naughty streak (why would you be anywhere else?) you can regularly make suggestions or take actions that push the boundaries of your intimate experiences further out. You'll have the dual satisfaction of exploring territory that you've not been to before, as well as taking the woman you're with to new and exciting heights – assuming she's not been there before! Even if she's been where you haven't, that's fine, since women that are really experienced and have had a full spectrum of sexual experiences truly appreciate a Good Bad Boy. They, more than most women, need to be with someone who is confident and really knows their way around, and isn't afraid to go there. Women generally aren't thrilled if they find they are more sexually experienced than the guy they are getting to know. Most women would rather not have to teach the guy, they want to be shown what skills you have – for them. So, as a fun example, the next romantic dinner that you're out at with your new partner, assuming you've both felt things out a bit, whisper in her ear, in a gentle but firm way, that you want her to go to the ladies room and remove her panties, and that she should bring them back for you to hold, and she'll have to make due without them for the rest of the evening. If she comes back with a clever reply, such as "why would you assume that I'm even wearing any?" make sure you keep your Good Bad Boy stature, and if she's wearing a dress or a skirt, you challenge her right then and there to surreptitiously prove it to you, as actions are what count. If she balks, you can be provocative and question the veracity of her statement. If she's wearing slacks, you will expect her to prove it later. Either way, you keep your balance. It's like volleying in tennis. Naughtiness in public is a huge turn on for many women. Don't be afraid to explore it, but don't be foolish or obvious either as it's a fine balance. Remember, there are many law enforcement personnel that will be less than amused by your activities if they catch you in the act. Oh, and be sure to put this woman right at the top of the list of your involvements – any woman who thinks that way is someone you want to know a *whole* lot more!

The only limitations are the ones that you put there, and if you both are adventuresome and playful, then let your minds roam and explore. All your practice at communication comes to fruition here, as discussions venture into the 'what turns you on' and 'what fantasies do you have' conversations. Of course you are matter of fact and unflappable regardless of what she says, assuming there is nothing illegal desired. I once had a woman ask me why I hadn't robbed a convenience store so she could fall in love with me. She may have been kidding but it didn't seem it at the time. Needless to say, that situation didn't get very far. As a Good Bad Boy I'm very accommodating, however, there are some boundaries that just won't be compromised.

Don't be afraid to push the envelope, and many times being spontaneous really helps. You are likely aware of the power of spontaneity romantically – bringing flowers or gifts, planning a special day for your girl and springing it on her, and so on. Sexual spontaneity has its own powerful space as well. You've established a safe place between you and your partner so don't be afraid to try new ideas. Obviously this can cover a lot of ground, but for starters, why not get a bit dominant with your woman. This doesn't mean getting disrespectful or speaking down to her, it's simply an extension of when you earlier learned how to really kiss, by making a woman feel a bit helpless when you did so, but now you're doing it in a bigger arena. Often a woman loves being overpowered sexually, and this can involve dozens of different scenarios. Luckily, it will take some time to sort through them all! Communicate and explore together, and a lot of fun discoveries will happen. A Good Bad Boy will try not to be shocked by a woman's behavior, in keeping with balance and stature, but how much fun it will be when a woman finally does take you aback. Acknowledge it, but don't be obvious about it!

Now it is time for the last part of your journey. How to carry all this knowledge, and yourself, through the rest of your life.

Chapter 9

Becoming the Good Bad Boyfriend/Husband

As time goes on and you travel further down the Good Bad Boy Path, you will have many wonderful experiences with many fabulous women, and if you stay on this path, you will earn a place in each one of their hearts, whether or not your relationships with these women are short or long term. Every connection has its own time span, whether it lasts seventy minutes or seventy years. The natural evolution of a Good Bad Boy at the end of all those cumulative experiences is to focus all that special knowledge on one very lucky and deserving woman. Sooner or later the seduction process, while a very satisfying experience, runs its course. It's an inevitable part of maturing, whether you have had your fill of it at 30 or at 50. From my experience and observation, men that are still not in committed relationships and pursuing and trying to seduce numbers of women into their 40's and 50's are not ever going to mature, and therefore have zero chance at becoming a Good Bad Boy. What their commitment issues are I'll leave to the psychologists, as our focus is on becoming the kind of man women adore, and ultimately become the object of adoration for one woman. The important thing to remember is, as a Good Bad Boy, you need to be with someone who appreciates and loves who you are and while she wants all that fun attention turned her way, does not want to change the tiger's stripes. Equally important for the Good Bad Boy is to be with a woman who not only appreciates who he is, but brings her own special attributes to the relationship.

Myself, I'm a very fortunate fellow in that the woman I'm with is beautiful and brilliant with a science PhD from MIT. There were many men that vied for her attentions that she could have chosen to have been with. Men with more money, more powerful careers, higher intelligence and so on. This is not to say I don't hold my own in all those departments, I do, but they had little to do with her selection. She initially was attracted by my look, but as we all know there needs to be more than that for things to last more than 5 minutes – at least in any relationship that matters. There are numerous times when I describe her to acquaintances who wonder how I ended up with someone of such significant substance. I just shrug my shoulders and toss up my hands in a 'beats me' type of way and joke that she hasn't come to her senses yet. All joking aside, what kept her close was my Good Bad Boy demeanor – letting Mr. Nice Guy have his place and being a Bad Boy when the time was called for. Apparently I also keep her in a state of perpetual amusement, but I think she just tells me that to make me feel less of a sex object.

It is very important to realize that just because you're committing to a deeper relationship doesn't mean that you're going to prison. Like everything else, a committed relationship has its plusses and minuses. As mentioned earlier, having the attentions of a lovely, decent woman who thinks you're the greatest thing since the invention of the wheel is one of the most valuable things you'll ever have in your possession. Being committed does not mean you stop being a Good Bad Boy; you just have to make your adjustments. Hopefully a big part of why you're in this relationship is that you share a lot in common, particularly when it comes to things in the realm of naughtiness. Being true to yourself is always a big part of the Good Bad Boy way, so now you just have to be a Good Bad Boy that is committed. There's nothing wrong with that at all. You still love women; still love flirting with them as you have before. As long as you reassure your partner that all your flirtatious behavior is not a reflection on how you feel about her, that no matter what you do you view your relationship with her as more important than anything.

It is important to discuss with her what the boundaries are as far as behavior. You may be very surprised as what will be ok with a woman, particularly one that has a Good Bad Boy as her significant other and feels that her relationship is solid. Remember, it was noted earlier that one of the most important things to a woman is emotional safety. She loves that you're a Good Bad Boy; she doesn't want that to change. She may be very turned on by hearing how while you were out picking up some milk from the store and almost picked up a cute woman while you were there as well. Maybe next time she'll want to go with you to see you in action! Who knows – you're only limited by what the two of you define as boundaries.

There is a Good Bad Boy friend of mine that is very happily married but of course takes the opportunity to flirt with a sexy woman whenever he gets the green light to do so. However, being a Good Bad Boy he would never lead a woman on, so he always makes sure to make mention of his wife shortly into the conversation. Most of the time that brings the flirtation to a quick but polite halt, but he has mentioned that is not always the case! Some women he has flirted with want to get to know him better, and when he mentions that he would never do anything without his wife, the adventurous woman offers that she'd like to meet her as well, so that there are no roadblocks and they can continue the flirtation. There are LOTS of open minded, adventurous women out there, so don't limit yourself by making assumptions. Just be a Good Bad Boy and be honest, and express how you feel. Just because you're committed or married doesn't mean the fun stops. All it means is that you have to handle things differently, because you now have different responsibilities. Maturity has its rewards!

<u>Now You Know, So Let It Go</u>

We've discussed many aspects of being a Good Bad Boy, but the most important one is being true to who you are. You never want to compromise yourself, do anything you don't really want to, or be reactive to the people or circumstances surrounding you. A huge part of what makes a Good Bad Boy so desirable is his solid sense of self. This separates the men from the boys. While women are more than happy to have a dalliance with a boy, being with a man is where the gold is. You will rarely be able to connect with a woman on a deep level if you do not carry yourself as a man and behave accordingly. Leave the boys and their behavior to the girls of the world. You're in this for much more rewarding pursuits, and being with a sexually open woman, as opposed to a girl who is sexually inexperienced and uncomfortable, is where you will always head to.

At the beginning of this journey you were likely someone who had desires and fantasies about how you wanted to interact sexually with women, but it seemed as accessible as jumping onto the surface of Mars. Now you are clear on who you are and what you want with the women in your life. You now can state your desires in a very palatable and seductive manner and not only have them heard and acknowledged, but more importantly have them fulfilled on a regular basis. As the fulfillment of your desires becomes more a part of your normal existence, the feelings that you would never get what you wanted sexually and that you had no power in this area or with women in general will disappear for good. Your confidence and self esteem will soar, yet throughout you are grateful and humble that you received the gift of this knowledge. You are cognizant that by being of service honoring the women in your life physically, emotionally, spiritually and simply being there for them, you also honor yourself as a man.

How To Be a Good Bad Boy

Now that you have all this heightened awareness, it is time to let it go. I'm sure you're wondering exactly what I'm talking about, and let's be regular guys one last time and use a sports analogy. In golf, you practice, practice, practice until your arms are ready to fall off, and when it's time to get on the course and play the game for real you must let all the thinking disappear. All that muscle memory must take over and the natural swing rhythm comes from somewhere deep within. I know every time I do a lot of thinking when I'm in the midst of a golf swing the results are almost always poor. Being a Good Bad Boy is the same. You've taken in all these points, and practiced trial and error and have reached a point where you have more than a clue on how to go about all of this. Of course, you'll have to think when trying to come up with a good reply or other conversation, but on the physical levels, it's time to let the natural rhythms you've developed take over from within. It always amazes me how the best golf shots seem to come from very little thought or physical effort. They come from within. As a Good Bad Boy expresses himself from the inside out, let everything come from within, naturally, without forethought or provocation. Eventually it will be as if you have a neon sign over your head, visible only to women in the world, quietly glowing 'Good Bad Boy' with a flashing arrow pointing down to you. The world will forever be a changed place.

When you first picked up this book, the thought of speaking to a woman in the tones discussed above, or to act in such a bold and sexual manner probably didn't even exist in your mind, it was so foreign. The point is now you know better; you know the power of behaving this way in an appropriate manner, and the rewards it will reap. You are only just finding out that there are many women out in the world that are hoping that today is the day they finally run into a guy who knows his stuff sexually, yet is humble and knows how to treat a woman like a woman – across the board. A guy who knows when to romance a woman and seduce her slowly and when to push her up against a wall and bring out the inner bad girl that she's been dying to let out, yet no man has been able to coax it out of her properly. A man who pushes the boundaries and doesn't hesitate to be spontaneous, naughty and adventuresome, yet at all times making sure the woman is right there with him. You'll know for certain when you've reached full Good Bad Boy status – you will never have to think of yourself that way, since the women in your life will be calling you a Good Bad Boy for you, just before they fall into your arms so you can do with them as you will – in that manner that only a Good Bad Boy knows how to do.

www.ingramcontent.com/pod-product-compliance
Lightning Source LLC
LaVergne TN
LVHW011422080426
835512LV00005B/220